Impact Investing

Finance Center for South-South Cooperation
Editor

Impact Investing

Global Trends and China's Practices

中国财经出版传媒集团
中国财政经济出版社

Springer

Editor
Finance Center for South-South Cooperation
Hong Kong, China

ISBN 978-981-99-4934-2 ISBN 978-981-99-4935-9 (eBook)
https://doi.org/10.1007/978-981-99-4935-9

Jointly published with China Financial & Economic Publishing House

This Springer imprint is published by the registered company Springer Nature Singapore Pte Ltd.
The registered company address is: 152 Beach Road, #21-01/04 Gateway East, Singapore 189721, Singapore

Preface

In September 2015, the United Nations proposed 17 sustainable development goals, with the tenet to thoroughly address the social, economic, and environmental problems confronting global development in an integrated manner from 2015 to 2030. As the concept of sustainable development gains widespread support, impact investing is increasingly attracting attention and becoming a hot topic both at home and abroad. In September 2020, when addressing the general debate of the 75th Session of the United Nations General Assembly, Chinese President Xi Jinping pledged to the international community to achieve "carbon maximum and carbon neutral." In March 2021, the Chinese government issued the 14th Five-Year Plan and the outline of the long-term goals for 2035, attaching emphasized importance to green transformation in all areas of economic and social development. Against this backdrop, investors are increasingly concerned about sustainable development and the coordinated development of investment, environment, and society, while impact investing is viewed as one of the crucial means of capital market to pursue global sustainable development. Albeit its full development on international level, impact investing in China is still in the embryonic stage of development despite its rapid growth. Also, little systematic research has been carried out on impact investing in China.

The Finance Center for South-South Cooperation (FCSSC), a non-profit organization based in Hong Kong, China, with special consultative status for the United Nations Economic and Social Council, has been focusing on impact investing for many years. FCSSC strongly supported the UNDP, UNEP, and other UN organizations in their joint establishing the United Nations Social Impact Fund and engaged in long-term, in-depth tracking of CD Finance, a successful case of China's impact investing.

This book, by reviewing international experiences and the Chinese practice of impact investing, aims to offer a more precise definition of impact investing, advocate the standardization of the measurement and evaluation system for impact investing, advance the establishment of China's impact investing ecosystem, and guide investment to place equal emphasis on social environmental impact and profit, the dual objectives. This book consists of four main parts: clarification of the definition of impact investing; systematical summary of the development process, characteristics, and trends of international impact investing; review of the current situation and features of impact investing in China; and an in-depth analysis of CD Finance, a successful case in impact investing in China.

This book is organized and edited by FCSSC. Special thanks go to the distinguished experts and scholars at home and abroad who participated in writing this book, including Dr. Han Jun (adjunct Professor at Georgetown University), Ms. Wu Yifei (Ph.D. candidate at Harvard Business School), Ms. Rae Winborn (Peking University), Prof. Yuan Ruijun (associate professor at the School of Government Peking University), Ms. Wang Dandan (US-based Scholar), and Mr. Liu Dongwen (CD Finance). I would also like to thank the editor-in-chief of this book, Dr. Liu Qianqian (Deputy Director General of FCSSC) for her great efforts in designing and managing the project and the book, organizing experts, external coordination, and Chinese and English editing. Finally, I would like to thank Mr. Pan Zhanfeng of FCSSC, Mr. Luo Yahong, Director of International Cooperative Publishing Center of China Financial and Economic Publishing House, his amazing colleague Ms. Gu Lei, and Ms. Liu Xinyu of CIPG. Without their great support and coordination, this book could not have been completed successfully.

Dr. Wu Zhong
Director General
Finance Center for South-South
Cooperation
Hong Kong, China

Contents

Abbreviations

AIMM	Anticipated Impact Measurement and Monitoring
AMAC	Asset Management Association of China
AUM	Assets Under Management
AVPN	Asian Venture Philanthropy Network
BOP	Base of the Pyramid
BSC	Big Society Capital
CAF	Charity Aid Foundation
CASVI	China Alliance of Social Value Investment
CBAC	Capacity Building Assessment Center
CBRC	China Banking Regulatory Commission
CDC	Center for Disease Control and Prevention
CDFI	Community Development Financial Institution
CFPA	China Foundation for Poverty Alleviation
CGAP	Consultative Group to Assist the Poor
CIC	Community Interest Company
CITR	Community Investment Tax Relief
CSEIF	China Social Enterprise and Impact Investment Forum
CSR	Corporate Social Responsibility
CSRC	China Securities Regulatory Commission
CSRDC	Corporate Social Responsibility Development Center
CZI	Chan Zuckerberg Initiative
DFI	Development Financial Institution
EMPEA	Emerging Markets Private Equity Association
ERISA	Employee Retirement Income Security Act of 1974
ESG	Environmental, Social and Governance
EVPA	European Venture Philanthropy Association
FIS	Fund for Social Innovation
FYSE	Foundation for Youth Social Entrepreneurship
GDP	Gross Domestic Product
GIIN	Global Impact Investing Network
GIIRS	Global Impact Rating System

GPI	Global Philanthropy Institute
GSFF	Global Social Finance Forum
GSG	Global Steering Group for Impact Investment
HICA	High Impact Capital Advisors
HIPSO	Harmonized Indicators for Private Sector Operation
HNWI	High Net Worth Individual
IDB	Inter-American Development Bank
IFC	International Finance Corporation
IIX	Impact Investment Exchange (Singapore)
IMM	Impact Multiple of Money
IMP	Impact Measurement Project
IRIS	Impact Reporting and Investment Standards
IRR	Internal Rate of Return
LGT	Liechtenstein Global Trust
LP	Limited Partner
MCC	Microcredit Company
MFI	Microfinance Institution
MIV	Microfinance Investment Vehicle
MIX	Microfinance Information Exchange
MRI	Mission-Related Investment
NAB	The US National Advisory Board on Impact Investing
NBFI	Non-Bank Financial Institution
NCFP	National Center for Family Philanthropy
NGO	Non-Governmental Organization
OECD	Organization for Economic Co-operation and Development
P2P	Peer to Peer
PBOC	People's Bank of China
PRI	Program-Related Investment
RCT	Randomized-Controlled Trial
RDD	Regression Discontinuity Design
ROA	Return on Asset
ROE	Return on Equity
SDG	Sustainable Development Goal
SE	Social Enterprise
SEAF	Small Enterprise Assistance Fund
SEIF	Social Enterprise Investment Fund
SERC	Social Enterprise Research Center
SIB	Social Impact Bond
SIPPRA	Social Impact Partnership to Pay for Results Act
SITR	Social Investment Tax Relief
SME	Small and Medium Enterprise
SOCAP	Social Capital Market
SOE	State Owned Enterprise
SPTF	Social Performance Task Force
SRI	Socially Responsible Investing

SROI	Social Return on Investment
SSA	Sub-Saharan Africa
SSE	Social Stock Exchange
SWE	Social Welfare Enterprise
TBLI Group	Triple Bottom Line Investing Group
TPG	Texas Pacific Group
UBS	United Bank of Switzerland
UFA	Universal Financial Access
UNCTAD	United Nations Conference on Trade and Development
UNDP	United Nations Development Programme
UNEP	United Nations Environment Programme
UNIDO	United Nations Industrial Development Organization
UNOSSC	United Nations Office for South-South Cooperation
UNSIF	UNDP SDG Innovative Finance
US SIF	US Sustainable and Responsible Investment Forum
VC	Venture Capital
VIE	Variable Interest Entity
WASH	Water, Sanitation and Hygiene
WBG	World Bank Group
WNS Europe	Western, Northern, and Southern Europe

Definition of Impact Investing

1 Definition of Impact Investing

Impact investing exists within a broader spectrum of investment based on financial and social returns. On one side of the investment spectrum, traditional financial investment seeks to maximize financial return with very limited or no regard for social impacts. On the other side of the spectrum, pure social investing, such as philanthropy, seeks only social returns with no financial return (Rockefeller Philanthropy Advisors 2017).

The authoritative definition of "impact investing" comes from the Global Impact Investing Network (GIIN). GIIN defines impact investing as "investments made with the intention to generate positive, measurable social and environmental impact alongside a financial return" (GIIN). The creation of the term dates back to 2007 when it was coined by the Rockefeller Foundation at a conference in its Bellagio Center in Italy (Han and Shah 2019). This event is usually regarded as the beginning of the modern age of impact investing.

According to GIIN, the core characteristics of impact investing practices include four aspects:

(1) "Intentionally contributing to positive social and environmental impact alongside a financial return;
(2) Using evidence and impact data in investment design;
(3) Managing impact performance;
(4) Contributing to the growth of impact investing" (GIIN 2019).

Based on GIIN's annual report, impact investments are channeled through the following asset classes:

(1) "Private debt: Bonds or loans placed to a select group of investors rather than being syndicated broadly.
(2) Public debt: Publicly traded bonds or loans.

Finance Center for South-South Cooperation, *Impact Investing*,
https://doi.org/10.1007/978-981-99-4935-9_1

(3) Equity-like debt: An instrument between debt and equity, such as mezzanine capital or deeply subordinated debt. Often a debt instrument with potential profit participation, such as convertible debt, warrant, royalty, debt with equity kicker.
(4) Private equity: A private investment into a company or fund in the form of an equity stake (not publicly traded stock).
(5) Public equity: Publicly traded stocks or shares.
(6) Real assets: An investment of physical or tangible assets as opposed to financial capital, such as real estate or commodities".

Since 2007, impact investment has grown rapidly. Recently, more and more similar terms related to impact investment have emerged. Some terms that often appear are sorted out here.

1.1 ESG

The term ESG (Environmental, Social and Governance) was first coined in 2004 in the report entitled "Who Cares Wins: Connecting Financial Markets to a Changing World" by the United Nations Global Compact. In 2006, the United Nations released the Principles for Responsible Investment (PRI) that "offer a menu of possible actions for incorporating ESG issues into investment practice" (UNEP Finance Initiative and UN Global Compact 2019). By 29 November 2021, the number of signatories of the PRI has grown from 100 to 4569, managing more than 80 trillion US dollars.[1]

In 2019, the World Bank Group launched the Sovereign ESG Data Portal, providing sovereign-level environmental, social, and governmental data. The ESG data platform comprises 17 themes that correspond to the 17 Sustainable Development Goals (SDGs) In the ESG data portal, the "E"—"environment"—includes (1) emissions and pollution, (2) natural capital endowment and management, (3) energy use and security, (4) environment/climate risk and resilience, and (5) food security. The "S"—"social"—includes (1) education and skills, (2) employment, (3) demography, (4) poverty and inequality, (5) health and nutrition, and (6) access to services. The "G"—"governance"—includes (1) human rights, (2) government effectiveness, (3) stability and the rule of law, (4) economic environment, (5) gender, and (6) innovation.

1.2 Social Investment

The definition of social investment comes from the Big Society Capital (BSC), the world's first social investment wholesale bank, founded in London in April 2012. The BSC has provided two versions of the definition of social investment. Before

[1] UNPRI, "Full list of PRI Signatories", https://www.unpri.org/signatories/signatory-resources/signatory-directory, November 29, 2021.

2019, BSC's definition of social investment was "repayable finance for charities and social enterprises that targets both financial and social returns for investors. Charities and social enterprises can use repayable finance to help them increase their impact on society by maintaining cash flow, buying an asset, growing, or kick-starting their organization. They can choose to access this finance from social investors, who will be motivated by their social missions. For investors, social investment is part of the spectrum of impact investment. It actively targets high-impact investments by focusing on charities and social businesses. Sometimes investors will accept lower returns or take greater risks to achieve this".

In 2019, the website of the BSC provided an updated version of the definition of social investment. "Essentially, social investment refers to repayable finance used to create social impact, mainly through social enterprises and charities. Social investing is a subset of impact investing, with some distinguishing factors including the intention to deliver deep impact, being impact first, and with a long-term commitment to delivering impact" (Big Society Capital 2019). Notably, social investments include investments in charities, while impact investing does not include investments in charities, which is probably the main difference between the two terms.

Impact investing is often used in the United States, while social investment is widely used in the United Kingdom. The two concepts have a large overlap, with minor differences. In fact, they are two different names of the same thing.

1.3 Social Impact Investment

"Social impact investing" is often used in the United States. "Social investment" is usually used in the United Kingdom. The two concepts are largely overlapped, with minor differences. In fact, they are two sides of the same coin.

"Social impact investment" combines the strengths of the two keywords—impact investment and social investment—by emphasizing the impact in the social domain. According to Social Impact Investment Taskforce, which was established at the 2013 G8 Social Impact Investment Forum, and superseded by the Global Social Impact Investment Steering Group (GSG) in 2015, social impact investments are "those that intentionally target specific social objectives along with a financial return and measure the achievement of both" (Nicholls et al. 2015).

1.4 Social Finance

Social finance is "the allocation of capital primarily for social and environmental returns, as well as in some cases, a financial return" (Nicholls et al. 2015). Within the broad definition, there exists a spectrum of diverse social finance approaches, spanning from a sole focus on social return on one end to a sole focus on financial return on the other (Nicholls et al. 2015).

According to *Challenges and Opportunities in Social Finance in the UK*, social finance incorporates a number of socially orientated financial activities, including:

(1) Impact investment—investing for both a financial return and a social return.
(2) Social banking—investing deposits in social enterprises.
(3) Charitable banking—banking with a specific focus on the needs of charities.
(4) Providing banking services and advice to financially excluded individuals.
(5) Crowdfunding platforms for funding social ventures (Howard 2012).

1.5 CSR and CSR Investing

Corporate Social Responsibility (CSR) is a management concept whereby companies integrate social and environmental concerns in their business operations and interactions with their stakeholders. CSR is generally understood as being the way through which a company achieves a balance of economic, environmental, and social imperatives (so-called "triple-bottom-line approach") while at the same time addressing the expectations of shareholders and stakeholders. CSR Investing is an investment in CSR activities.

1.6 Socially Responsible Investing (SRI)

Socially responsible investing means avoiding investing in industries that negatively affect the environment and people. This includes companies that produce or invest in alcohol, tobacco, gambling, and weapons. Instead, SRI involves investing in companies engaged in ethical and socially conscious themes, like environmental sustainability and social justice.

1.7 Venture Philanthropy

Venture Philanthropy (VP) is a high-engagement and long-term approach whereby an investor for impact supports a social purpose organization (SPO) to help it maximize its social impact. The term venture philanthropy emphasizes supporting social purpose organizations and excludes for-profit organizations.

1.8 Blended Finance

According to the GIIN 2018 Annual Survey, blended finance is "a strategy that combines capital with different levels of risk in order to catalyze risk-adjusted, market-rate-seeking capital into impact investments" (Mudaliar et al. 2018). The World Economic Forum and Organization for Economic Co-operation and Development (OECD) define blended finance as "the strategic use of development finance and philanthropic funds to mobilize private capital flows to emerging and frontier markets" (OECD and World Economic Forum 2015). Blended finance "deliberately channels private investment to sectors of high-development impact while at the same time delivering risk-adjusted returns" (OECD and World Economic Forum 2015). It "attempts to achieve similar goals to Impact Investing (intentional approach to create societal and financial impacts) by using a structuring approach to "blend" the different intents of a range of investor motivations to achieve these development objectives at scale" (OECD and World Economic Forum 2015).

Recent industry terminology suggests that while impact investing, sustainable investing, ESG investing, and SRI are all impact-generating investment strategies, they have important differences. There are two critical elements of impact investing that can distinguish it from other investments:

- **Intentionality**. To solve a particular problem and achieve a particular social or environmental goal is equally important as financial return, not just for the benefit of financial return. As GIIN (2019) pointed out, "impact investors aim to solve problems and address opportunities. This is at the heart of what differentiates impact investing from other investment approaches (such as ESG investing and Socially Responsible Investing), which may incorporate impact considerations."
- **Measurement for societal and environmental impacts**. Impact investors need to know exactly where the money is going and what it is used for, measure the impacts of investments, and report to the investor with specific metrics. As GIIN (2019) pointed out, "impact investing is marked by an intentional desire to contribute to measurable social or environmental benefit."

Sustainable investing, SRI, and ESG investment approaches include a broad spectrum ranging from negative screening (avoiding investing in business that are counter to investor's values) to positive screening (pursuing positive social or environmental outcomes). However, they still focus on financial return as the end goal and they seek to achieve positive social and environmental outcomes for the benefit of financial returns (Boffo and Patalano 2020). ESG factors are utilized to help assess business risk and improve business practices, which in turn can improve market valuations and financial performance.

Impact investing is much more proactive and intentional in pursuing specific and measurable societal and environmental impacts, which are important end goals as adequate financial return. Because the financial returns continued to be the dominant focus of SRI and ESG investment, which are "not well-suited to support the creation of cutting-edge solutions for society's neglected issues and segments" (Singh 2020), the term of impact investing was created to fill in the gap and to distinguish a group of investors who intentionally pursue measurable social impacts. Impact investing goes much further than SRI and ESG investment "in terms of defining, measuring, and managing the precise societal impact while striving to generate financial returns" (Singh 2020). In terms of expectations for financial return, impact investors include

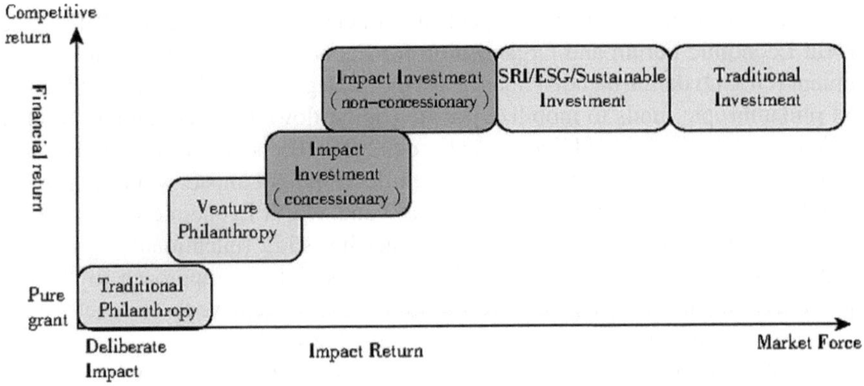

Fig. 1 Position of impact investment. *Source* Jasjit Singh. Maximising Outcomes in Impact Investing (2020)

"concessionary investors who are willing to make some financial sacrifice by taking greater risks or accepting lower returns to achieve social goal" (Brest and Born 2013), and "non-concessionary investors who are not willing to make any financial sacrifice to achieve their social goals" (Brest and Born 2013). Figure 1 illustrates where impact investing sits within the investment spectrum and how it differs from philanthropy, SRI, and ESG investment in terms of social and financial return.

2 Definition of Impact Investing in the Chinese Context

As stated by the Global Impact Investing Network (GIIN), "For impact investments to contribute effectively to positive social and environmental impacts and for the approach to remain credible, the financial markets need clarity on expected practice and the terms of participation in the impact investing market." Without an agreed-upon standard for impact investing, investors will be unable to compare their financial and social returns and thus cannot provide conclusive proof of its effectiveness.

While a standard definition of impact investing is still up for debate globally, there is even less agreement around a prevailing definition in China. Lesley Gu, Business Division Director of China Alliance of Social Value Investment (CASVI), noted, "In China, lots of people claim to be impact investing, but few actually know how to be impact investors. They lack the evaluation standards."

The first reason for this is a general lack of awareness and basic understanding of the global definition of impact investing in China's non-profit and for-profit sectors. As Tan Yi, Program Manager of Narada Foundation, noted, "Those that know about impact investing have usually heard about it abroad and returned to China, so very few really understand it. There are a lot of people who put ESG (Environment, Social, and Governance), impacting investing, and SRI (Socially Responsible Investing) together, but Narada believes impact investing is not the same and shouldn't be lumped together." This lack of differentiation is perhaps understandable given readily available information about impact investing in China is inaccurate. For instance, the Baidu Baike definition equates impact investing and venture philanthropy, and a 2019 Zhihu query asking "What are some good impact investing organizations in China?" received mostly venture philanthropy organizations as examples. On the other extreme, a Sohu entry on impact investing uses ESG and socially responsible investment under the umbrella of impact investing.[2]

Indeed, over half of the interviewees indicated that a lack of understanding or confusion around the definition of impact investing was a major challenge facing the ecosystem. Several of the fund managers who indicated it was not an issue only raised capital from international investors and avoided local investors all together.

In addition, the translation of "impact investing" adds another layer of perplexity. Impact investing is usually literally translated as "social impact investing," but "social impact" does not hold the same meaning as it would in English; neither the translation for "social" nor "impact" allude to having a positive effect on one's community. YouChange, a foundation supporting impact investing in China, has pushed for an alternative translation, "social value investment," as they believe it is easier for Chinese people to understand (YouChange 2016). However, this definition is less widely used.

It is also important to note while many interviewees acknowledged the GIIN definition of impact investing, very few self-proclaimed impact investors have made impact investments as defined by GIIN. According to our analysis, impact investments in China total less than a hundred compared to GIIN's estimated 801 impact investments made globally in 2018 alone (Mudaliar et al. 2019).[3] Even fewer of these investors have successfully exited companies and generated positive revenue.

Interestingly, the most active advocates for impact investing are non-profit foundations, including the China Global Philanthropy Institute, China Social Enterprise and Impact Investment Forum, Asian Venture Philanthropy Network, Leping Foundation, YouChange, and Narada Foundation. While some organizations may have made a few impact investments (perhaps most notable is Narada's investment in Ehong Capital as a limited partner, or LP); the majority of these organizations are making a combination of grants and venture philanthropy investments. Reports often use venture philanthropy and impact investing interchangeably or lump them together as impact investing (YouChange 2016 Report; CSEIF and Narada 2019 Report). There are also several venture philanthropy funds and grant-making foundations that are potentially looking to expand into impact investing.

Previous international supporters may have also influenced the ecosystem early on and to push the ecosystem toward the venture philanthropy approach. The British

[2] Baidu Baike, (https://baike.baidu.com/item/%E5%BD%B1%E5%93%8D%E5%8A%9B%E6%8A%95%E8%B5%84/12016202?fr=aladdin); Zhihu (https://www.zhihu.com/question/24813068); Sohu (https://www.sohu.com/a/314020375_655147).

[3] Range is due to whether or not to count all of the known Tsing Capital investments, who started as a traditional investor 2000 and began to self-identify as an impact investor only much later. Breakout of investments made before and after this change is unknown.

Council was very active in assisting and training social entrepreneurs from 2009 to 2016 through its Social Enterprise Programme. Unlike most impact investors, the British Council advocates for a stricter definition of social enterprises, requiring social enterprises to reinvest all or most of their profits into their social mission (British Council). Thus, many of their social enterprises are more non-profit and community-focused rather than profit-seeking businesses.

The domination of non-profits and venture philanthropists and the early influence of international supporters in the impact investing and social enterprise field may have skewed the perspective of impact investing toward more philanthropic ideals. As Wei Fang, Executive Director of Ehong Capital, explained, "People still think that impact is about grants and philanthropy, and people think that impact-driven impact investing is more like impact investing." Thus, while the conversation around impact investing in China is changing rapidly, it has historically originated from the non-profit perspective rather than an investor perspective. This has blurred the differentiation between impact investing and venture philanthropy.

Finally, some local organizations may consider government investments as impact investments, adding to the confusion around what classifies as impact investing. Given the government's outsized role in most aspects of China's economy, the inclusion of government investment as impact investing is not surprising. Per a 2016 YouChange report, "The Chinese government, though it hasn't classified its assets by social impact investment, has, in fact, made a lot of social impact investment." YouChange includes loans granted by the China Development Bank and the Agricultural Bank of China and public–private partnerships as impact investments. Additionally, municipal governments have often incorporated venture philanthropy strategies, including the Shanghai Bureau of Civil Affairs' venture philanthropy competition in 2009 and its USD 750,000 fund (Zhao 2012).

Indeed, investments made by the government have many characteristics of venture philanthropy and impact investing: investments are made in projects and companies in order to reach social benchmarks, often at a lower or no market-rate return, and more commonly at a loss. While such activity is undoubtedly impactful, most would not fit under the definition of GIIN's impact investing as these investments are policy-driven or qualify as development finance. Per GIIN's definition, "development finance can be seen differently from impact investing in that it intends to create broad-based economic development (through boosting the economies of developing countries) but does not always necessarily intend to address or solve specific social or environmental challenges" (Mudaliar and Dithrich 2019).

A dearth of education around the global definition of impact investing, combined with difficulties in translation, a lack of distinction between venture philanthropy and impact investing in practice, and the outsized influence of government investments on the Chinese economy have all contributed to a muddled understanding of impact investing among varying stakeholders in the industry.

In the following sections, we will use the GIIN definition in order to understand how China's ecosystem compares to the rest of the world. However, it is clear that definitional clarity within China is needed if impact investing is ever to become a formalized industry. Given the unique circumstances surrounding how people in

China understand impact investing, it is necessary to address whether a localized definition is required. Casting a wider net to include venture philanthropy, ESG, and/or government investments has the benefit of inflating the market. In fact, this was the thinking behind the broad scope of the original 2007 impact investing definition proposed by the Rockefeller Foundation. However, this also has negative consequences, including further confusion. Again, this is something that the global impact investing community has struggled with and is attempting to fix through a tighter definition) Using the global definition of impact investing could serve as an anchor that can focus resources while leaving space for varying views. As Tan Yi of Narada Foundation argues, "Currently, China's impact investing space is not very mature or developed. Different people have different definitions of impact investing that is evolving quickly. Developing the industry is most important."

Apart from impact investing, there is also some ambiguity around other social impact terminology. It is important to distinguish impact investing from similar financial products and strategies that consider social impact. Impact investing's goals are different from these other financial products, and so it would be unfair and unhelpful to compare these products using impact investing standards.

As mentioned previously, many see venture philanthropy as indistinguishable from impact investing. ESG and socially responsible investing are also often lumped together with impact investing. Finally, the definition of social enterprises is not as well defined as it is in the West. "Social" is not associated with addressing social issues and "enterprise" is not associated with innovation in English. Because of this, there are three commonly used translations in Chinese: "social enterprise," "social start-up," and "social-start up for the public good" (FYSE 2012). While there is consensus around a basic definition that social enterprises are businesses with a social purpose achieved through integrating business strategies with social goals, there is no agreement on key characteristics of social enterprises (Lee 2012).

On the other hand, there are a few social impact terms that are China-specific. For instance, while the West has taken a bottom-up approach in defining "green finance" and has effectively let markets decide and innovate around the concept, China has taken a top-down approach. The government established guidelines for a green financial system in 2016. Globally, green finance is broadly defined as the "financing of investments that provide environmental benefits in the broader context of environmentally sustainable development" (G20 Green Finance Study Group 2016). The People's Bank of China (PBOC) issued specific criteria and standards for green bonds and green credit standards In China. Of course, there is still a lack of consensus around these standards (there are currently two sets of standards and performance disclosure is still incomplete), but policymakers are pushing toward clarification (Yao 2018). The term social welfare enterprise (SWE) is another concept that is uniquely Chinese. Under Chinese law, these are profit-seeking enterprises that employ at least 35% of disabled workers (Ministry of Civil Affairs 1990).

Because of this confusion between terminology, we will use the global definitions outlined in the previous section and provide a glossary in the appendix.

3 Outline and Methodology of the Book

3.1 Research Outline and Scope

This book consists of four main parts: clarification of the definition of impact investing; systematical summary of the development process, characteristics, and trends of international impact investment; review of the current situation and features of impact investment in China; and an in-depth analysis of CD Finance, a successful case in impact investment in China.

As outlined in the previous section, we will rely on the GIIN definition of impact investing, given it is the most widely-cited definition. However, while the GIIN definition includes investments that only return principal, we will only include investments that expect financial returns beyond principal. We also recognize the importance of both venture philanthropy and grants in building the impact investing ecosystem in China, as well as developing the continuum of social capital. While venture philanthropy is mentioned within the context of impact investing, we do not consider it impact investing and is not included in our market sizing and analysis. This definition will allow us to narrow the focus to impact investing firms that are most likely to attract traditional investor capital.

In addition, we have limited the scope by geography, institutional quality, and asset class in order to provide a more targeted and more in-depth analysis. First, we will focus only on activity in mainland China. Additionally, this report only includes institutional investments (e.g. through professional investment managers or institutions rather than direct investments made by private individuals) in order to get a clearer picture of the growth of impact investing as a professional industry. Finally, we have focused mainly on private equity and debt investments rather than public equity or bonds. This is mainly due to the fact that the majority of investments are allocated through private equity and debt vehicles, and thus the analysis will concentrate on the area that is most active.

3.2 Data Collection

In order to understand the impact investing ecosystem in China, semi-structured interviews were conducted with over 30 professionals involved in impact investing and venture philanthropy in mainland China, including representatives from local and international impact investors, foundations, social enterprises, industry organizations, and municipal government projects.[4] Participants detailed their firm's individual experiences as well as their thoughts on the future outlook of the industry.[5]

In addition to qualitative interviews, we also collect the general information of the main historic and active impact investing firms investing in mainland China, gathering primary sources (press releases, websites) and secondary sources. The relevant information also includes investment focus, donor profile, whether they were local or international, headquarters, founder background, and impact measurement system. The investment count has subsequently been used to size the market in the Development of Impact Investing in China and Current State in chapter three. Note that this is likely an undercount given some firms did not disclose their investment information, but it does give a general scale of the market.

3.3 Analytical Framework

We used a modified version of the Impact Investing Ecosystem Framework (Rivera Acevedo and Wu 2018) for our underlying analysis. This framework considers six domains within the impact investing ecosystem: finance, policy, markets, culture, supports, and human capital (see Fig. 2).

While previous frameworks such as the Organization for Economic Cooperation and Development (OECD) framework (OECD 2015) combine many different key factors (including social systems, tax laws, and financial markets) under "enabling factors," Rivera Acevedo and Wu divide these unique factors into separate groups. This ensures that important enabling environmental influences are not omitted. In addition, this framework relies more on interacting actors rather than performance and measurement, which is unavailable in early-stage ecosystems such as impact investing (Rivera Acevedo and Wu 2018). It also uses more general characteristics rather than relying on specific measures, which allows more flexibility to select appropriate indicators.

Through this approach, China's impact investing ecosystem can be comprehensively analyzed and compared to the global market, as well as individual country markets. Main factors influencing the industry can be identified, as well as key challenges and opportunities.

---

[4] Due to the limited actors directly involved in impact investing, the scope of interviewee participants was expanded to organizations using venture philanthropy and those interested and/or planning to do impact investing. We also interviewed organizations supporting impact investing through knowledge transfer, networking, and/or education. This expansion provides more context to the current state of impact investing and its potential.

[5] Example questionnaires are provided for each category of interviewee in the appendix.

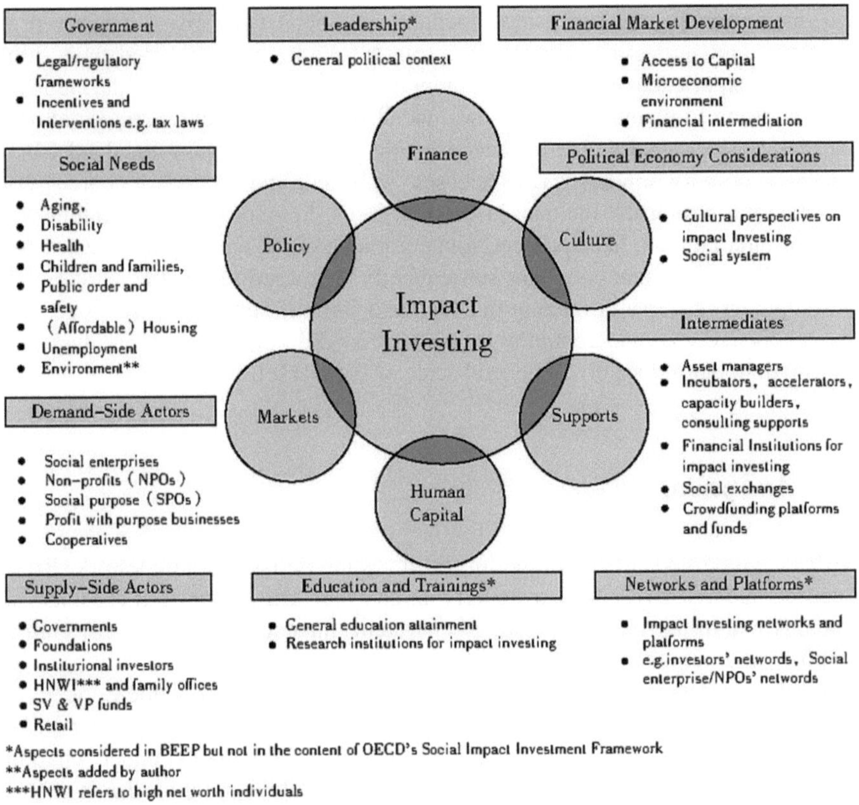

Fig. 2 Impact investing ecosystem framework. *Source* Rivera Acevedo and Wu (2018)

4 Contributions to the Book

This book contributes to the existing landscape literature in three distinct ways.

Firstly, this chapter takes a market-based perspective/investor-oriented perspective on impact investing. While existing reports imply that impact investing is useful mainly as a source of capital for social projects, organizations, or companies, we examine impact investing's potential to unlock private, financially motivated capital. This investor-focused approach allows us to investigate the market potential of impact investing and its scalability.

Secondly, this book provides a framework to comprehensively and systematically analyze the impact investing ecosystem in China. By building on existing frameworks used to analyze other impact investing markets, our analysis will allow for easier comparison to impact investing globally.

Thirdly, this book has helped outline the general picture of the historic and current impact investing in China. Our methodology is based on extensive practitioner interviews and firm-level investment information. By collecting quantitative resources, as well as qualitative information from practitioners on the ground, we can provide a complete picture of impact investing in China as it stands today. Furthermore, this book could provide a foundation for further research and data collection and potentially be used for more empirical research in the future.

References

Boffo R, Patalano R (2020) ESG investing: practices, progress and challenges. www.oecd.org/finance/ESG-Investing-Practices-Progress-and-Challenges.pdf

Brest P, Born K (2013) Unpacking the impact in impact investing. Stanf Soc Innov Rev. https://ssir.org/articles/entry/unpacking_the_impact_in_impact_investing

China Social Enterprise and Impact Investment Forum and Narada Foundation (2019) China Social Enterprise and Social Investment Landscape Report 2019. China Social Enterprise and Impact Investment Forum and Narada Foundation.

Foundation for Youth Social Entrepreneurship (2012) 2012 China Social Enterprise Report.

GIIN (2019) Core characteristics of impact investing. https://thegiin.org/assets/Core%20Characteristics_webfile.pdf

G20 Green Finance Study Group (2016) G20 green finance synthesis report. G20 Green Finance Study Group

Han J, Shah S (2019) The ecosystem of scaling social impact: a new theoretical framework and two case studies. J Soc Entrep 1–25

Howard E (2012) Challenges and opportunities in social finance in the UK, Cicero Group. https://apsocialfinance.files.wordpress.com/2013/01/2012-challenges-opportunities-in-uk-sf.pdf

Lee R (2012) The emergence of social enterprises in China: the quest for space and legitimacy. Tsinghua China Law Rev 2(79):80–99

Ministry of Civil Affairs (1990) Interim measures for the administration of social welfare enterprises

Mudaliar A, Dithrich H (2019) Sizing the impact investing market. The GIIN. https://thegiin.org/research/publication/impinv-market-size. Accessed 31 July 2019

Mudaliar A, Bass R, Dithrich H (2018) Annual impact investor survey. GIIN. https://thegiin.org/research/publication/annualsurvey2018

Mudaliar A et al (2019) Annual impact investor survey. GIIN. https://thegiin.org/research/publication/impinv-survey-2019

Nicholls A, Paton R, Emerson J (eds) (2015) Social finance. Oxford University Press, Oxford

OECD and World Economic Forum (2015) Blended finance vol. 1: a primer for development finance and philanthropic funders. http://www3.weforum.org/docs/WEF_Blended_Finance_A_Primer_Development_Finance_Philanthropic_Funders.pdf

Rivera Acevedo J, Wu M (2018) A proposed framework to analyze the impact investing ecosystem in a cross-country perspective. Rev Eur Stud 10(4):87–113

Rockefeller Philanthropy Advisor (2017) Impact investing introduction. https://www.rockpa.org/wp-content/uploads/2017/10/RPA_PRM_Impact_Investing_Intro_WEB.pdf

Singh J (2020) Maximising outcomes in impact investing. INSEAD knowledge. https://knowledge.insead.edu/strategy/maximising-outcomes-in-impact-investing-13636?page=2&page=2&page=1&

UNEP Finance Initiative and UN Global Compact (2019) Principles for responsible investment. https://www.unpri.org/download?ac=6303

Yao W (2018) China's green finance strategy: much achieved, further to go. London School of Economics Grantham Research Institute on Climate Change and the Environment. 24 October. http://www.lse.ac.uk/GranthamInstitute/news/chinas-green-finance-strategy-much-achieved-further-to-go/

YouChange China Social Entrepreneur Foundation and China Development Research Foundation (2016) China Social Impact Investment Report 2016. YouChange China Social Entrepreneur Foundation, China Development Research Foundation.
Zhao M (2012) The social enterprise emerges in China. Stanf Soc Innov Rev 10(2)

A Brief History and Current Development of Impact Investing Globally

Impact investing emerged as a new type of investment in the past decades probably due to two reasons. Firstly, in a larger sense, the emergence of impact investment is a reaction to the negative consequences of capitalism or neoliberalism. The negative consequences include but are not limited to growing income inequality, poverty, unemployment, racial and gender inequity, disparity in health and education outcomes, and many other social problems. Impact investments emerged in its inner heart to respond to these rising economic and social issues.

Secondly, as impact investing has gained wide recognition in recent years, it is important to note that the ideas and approaches associated with impact investment have existed in various forms over a long period time. Initially, investors mindful of social responsibility pursued the fulfillment of social values by intentionally avoiding making investments in products or activities with negative social effects, such as weapons, alcohol, tobacco, or gambling. In the 1980s and 1990s, academics, international organizations, and investors began tossing around the idea of actively creating social values through investment instead of avoiding investing in negative things. They believed that investing with social impact does not necessarily require sacrificing financial return. Instead, investment can generate both financial and social returns. By doing so, investors consider a wider range of factors in building their investment portfolios, such as corporate social responsibility and other intangible assets a firm builds in addition to tangible, financial ones. Furthermore, severe reflections on social problems and the reformist potentials of capitalism in the wake of financial crises have propelled additional efforts to formalize the definition and strategies for impact investments.

To demonstrate how impact investment evolved, this section provides an overview of major events that occurred in the modern history of impact investment, that is from 2007 to the present. It highlights key players, leading organizations, and best practices that appeared in modern history.

Finance Center for South-South Cooperation, *Impact Investing*,
https://doi.org/10.1007/978-981-99-4935-9_2

1 The History of Impact Investing Globally

The beginning of the modern age of impact investment is well recognized in 2007, when the Rockefeller Foundation proposed the term "Impact Investing" at a conference it convened in Bellagio, Italy, for the first time. In the second year, Pierre Omidyar, the founder of eBay, launched the Omidyar Network, a philanthropic investment company co-founded by Pierre and his wife Pam, to start making impact investments. The Omidyar Network is one of the prominent pioneers in impact investments.

The year 2009 witnessed several significant progress. In June 2009, the UK Department of Health and Social Care established the Social Enterprise Investment Fund, focusing on impact investment in health-related social enterprises. In July 2009, the Global Impact Investing Network (GIIN) was launched, and later the GIIN created Impact Reporting and Investment Standards (IRIS). The GIIN gradually became an infrastructure organization for the entire industry of impact investment, especially in the United States. In December 2009, the White House under the Obama Administration opened the Office of Social Innovation and Civic Participation. This office is the highest level of government agency in the world that was founded to support impact investments, social innovation, and civic engagement.

In 2010, progresses continued. In the legal framework, Maryland in the United States passed the first Benefit Corporation legislation in April 2010. By the end of 2019, 33 states in the United States had passed this legislation, and eight states were considering the pass. The Benefit Corporation legislation created a new legal category for social enterprises to formally register in the United States, and social enterprises are ideal entities to receive impact investments.

In June 2010, the Social Investment Forum was launched with the mission to promote sustainable and responsible investing in the United States. In June 2011, the forum was renamed as the US Sustainable and Responsible Investment Forum (US SIF). US SIF gradually became one of the infrastructure organizations for impact investment.

British then Prime Minister Cameron announced the scheme of "Big Society" in 2010. The Big Society Scheme is one of the most well-known policies to support the social sector. It highlighted the role of impact investments and social enterprises in addressing pressing social issues and social demands.

In August 2010, the first Social Impact Bond (SIB) was launched in London. The first SIB aims to reduce reoffending rates or recidivism among short-sentenced offenders in the United Kingdom while generating financial returns for impact investors. SIB gradually became a popular financial mechanism in impact investment in the following years.

In November 2010, JP Morgan Chase and the Rockefeller Foundation jointly released the report, *Impact Investments: An Emerging Asset Class*. This report defines impact investment as a new asset class, compared with venture capital and private equity. The report identified potential investment opportunities between $400 billion to $1 trillion in the years from 2010 to 2020.

In 2011, intermediary organizations and industry standards of impact investment were developing. In March 2011, the GIIN launched ImpactBase. ImpactBase is a global directory of impact investments. ImpactBase has listed 5220 accredited impact investors subscribers and 440 active impact investment funds. This is the first directory of impact investors. In September 2011, the B Lab, a nonprofit that created the B Corporation certification for for-profit organizations, launched Global Impact Investing Rating System (GIIRS). The GIIRS (pronounced "gears") is a comprehensive and transparent system for assessing the social and environmental impact of developed and emerging market companies and funds. It became one of the prominent criteria of assessing social impact for impact investors.

As a part of the Big Society Scheme, in April 2012, the Big Society Capital (BSC) was launched in London as the world's first wholesale social investment bank. BSC was financed with an estimated £600 million of equity to be paid in over five years. £400 million is from unclaimed assets left in dormant bank accounts for over 15 years, and £200 million is committed from big four British banks (Barclay, HSBC, Lloyds, and the Royal Bank of Scotland).

In August 2012, the first U.S. social impact bond was released in New York to support the delivery of therapeutic services to 16 to 18-year-old incarcerated persons on Rikers Island (Olson and Phillips 2013). The first SIB in the United States was operated by Social Finance US, a sister organization of Social Finance UK, and supported by Goldman Sachs, Bloomberg Philanthropies, the New York City Mayor's Office and the Department of Correction, the Osborne Association, and Friends of Island Academy.

The legal frameworks and the global and country alliances of impact investments made further development in 2013. In January 2013, the UK's Public Service Act or Social Value Act came into effect after decades of deliberation. The Act calls for all public sector commissioning to factor in social, economic, and environmental well-being in connection with public services contracts. It supports impact investments and social enterprises in bidding government contracts, assessing the overall social and environmental impact, rather than only considering the lowest price in the commissioning. In June 2013, following the recommendations of the G8 Task Force on Impact Investing, the National Advisory Board (NAB) was founded in the United States. It was led by Omidyar Network and Social Finance US to craft a U.S. domestic policy agenda around impact investing. In 2017, The NAB was rebranded as the U.S. Impact Investing Alliance. The Alliance aims to continue catalyzing the impact investing movement in the United States. In September 2013, the B Lab created B Analytics. B Analytics is a customizable data platform for measuring, benchmarking, and reporting on social impact. It is a useful online instrument for impact investors to identify investment opportunities.

In February 2014, Sonal Shah, former director of the White House Office of Social Innovation and Civic Participation, became the founding director of the Beeck Center for Social Impact and Innovation at Georgetown University. The Beeck Center is dedicated to fostering collaboration, innovation as well as pragmatic and experiential learning across the social sector, particularly on impact investment, social innovation, technology, and governance.

The U.K. government introduced Social Investment Tax Relief (SITR) in April 2014. The SITR was designed to provide tax relief to impact investors to encourage impact investments and help social enterprises attract capital to grow their businesses. In June 2014, the Obama Administration convened 20 leading U.S. private-sector investors at the White House to pledge $1.5 billion in commitments to impact investments. This is another example of how the government can support impact investment.

In July 2014, the China Social Enterprise and Impact Investment Forum (CSEIF) was launched to foster dialogues and cross-border exchanges and to promote the development of social enterprises and impact investments in China. In 2017, China Social Enterprise and Impact Investment Forum started to announce the Social Impact Awards to social enterprises and impact investors.

In September 2014, the Impact Investment Taskforce chaired by Sir Ronald Cohen released the report, *Impact Investment: The Invisible Heart of Market*. This report called for governments and the financial sector to utilize billions of funds from charitable trusts, pension funds, and wealth funds to promote impact investments. In October 2014, Giving Pledge, sponsored by Warren Buffett, Bill Gates, and Melinda Gates, set up the Impact Investing Affinity Group to share their experience in impact investment. Giving Pledge is a network of leading impact investors that emerged in the United States, and afterward spread to the world.

In February 2015, the BlackRock Global Impact Fund was launched. It seeks to maximize long-term total returns through active investment in global companies whose core business products or services are addressing the world's greatest social and environmental problems as identified by the UN Sustainable Development Goals (SDGs). As of 2016, the platform managed $200 billion in assets across impact investing and environment, social, and governance (ESG) portfolios.

Cambridge Associates and the GIIN launched the Impact Investing Benchmark in June 2015. The Benchmark is a comprehensive analysis of the financial performance of market-rate private equity and venture capital impact funds, with social impact objectives. In August 2015, the Group Steering for Global Impact Investment (GSG) was established as the successor to the G8 Impact Investment Taskforce established under the UK's presidency of the G8. The GSG currently has 32 countries plus the EU as members, chaired by Sir Ronald Cohen. GSG and GIIN are two leading networks or infrastructure organizations for impact investments, based in the United Kingdom and United States, respectively.

The United Nations proposed the Sustainable Development Goals (SDGs) in September 2015. The Rockefeller Foundation estimated that meeting the SDGs would cost between $50 trillion and $70 trillion. In October 2015, the U.S. Department of Labor provided regulatory guidelines that expanded the use of environmental, social, and governance (ESG) investing principles under the Employee Retirement Income Security Act (ERISA). In December 2015, the Chan Zuckerberg Initiative (CZI) was registered as a limited liability company (LLC) by Facebook founder Mark Zuckerberg and his wife Priscilla Chan with an investment of "up to $1 billion in Facebook shares in each of the next three years." The goal of CZI is to "advance human potential and promote equality in areas such as health, education, scientific research, and energy". CZI is a prominent player in impact investment, especially in health, education, energy, and scientific research.

In April 2016, the U.S. Treasury Department and IRS released guidance clarifying how private foundations can use increasingly popular Program-Related Investments (PRI) to maximize their social impact. PRIs are investments made by a foundation to pursue its charitable mission rather than to generate income. The emergence of PRIs further supports the development of impact investment in the United States.

The China Alliance of Social Value Investment (CASVI) was established as a Chinese network of impact investors in September 2016. At the same time, the China Charity Fair announced the certification of social enterprises in China. A total of 16 social enterprises were certificated for the first time in China. The two events targeting the upstream and downstream of impact investments respectively occurred in the same month. In November 2016, the Narada Foundation in China launched a platform to accelerate the scaling of social goods.

In April 2017, the Ford Foundation announced it would commit up to $1 billion from its $12 billion endowments over the next ten years to the nascent investment field known as Mission-Related Investing. A mission-related investment (MRI) is broadly defined as a financial investment that also furthers an organization's mission. Both MRIs and PRIs are characterized by an intention to create positive social impact as well as some level of financial return, but unlike PRIs, MRIs do not need to meet a specific charitable standard.

The Case Foundation launched the beta version of the Impact Investing Network Map in June 2017. It is an interactive online instrument showcasing the publicly available transactions between companies and investors within Impact Investing. This instrument makes impact investment visible online.

Japan's Government Pension Investment Fund (GPIF), the world's largest pension fund, announced that it had allocated 1 trillion yen ($8.9 billion) of funds to socially responsible investments in July 2017. This means the World's largest pension fund started to make impact investments.

In November 2017, a group of leading philanthropists including Bill and Melinda Gates, Jeffery Skoll, and the Rockefeller Foundation announced the formation of Co-Impact (Co-Impact.org). Co-Impact plans to invest US $500 million in three critical areas—health, education, and economic opportunity—to improve the lives of underserved populations across the developing world.

The first China Global Social Finance Forum and Social Impact Investing Summit was held in Shenzhen in December 2017. The China Charity Fair announced new certificated social enterprises in China—a total of 106 social enterprises were certificated. In the same month, the China Alliance of Social Value Investment (CASVI) released the Social Value Assessment Report on A-share listed companies.

The United States passed the 2017 Tax Cuts and Jobs Act, in which Opportunity Zones were created to drive long-term capital into low-income communities in December 2017. The policy of Opportunity Zone uses tax incentives to encourage private investment into designated census tracts through privately or publicly managed investment funds. In June 2018, the U.S. Treasury had approved Opportunity Zones in all 50 U.S. states, five territories, and Washington, District of

Columbia. This is a prominent example that the U.S. government encourages and supports impact investments.

BlackRock founder and CEO Larry Fink published his annual letter, *A Fundamental Reshaping of Finance* in January 2018. His letter urges CEOs and companies to position the long-term profitability of their businesses by keeping their focus on the role of the corporation in society. This letter captured wide attention and promoted the trend of impact investment.

In February 2018, the Social Impact Partnerships to Pay for Results Act (SIPPRA) was signed into law in the United States. The U.S. Congress appropriated $100 million for the SIPPRA program to implement "Social Impact Partnership Demonstration Projects" and feasibility studies to prepare for these projects. The SIPPRA program is administered by the U.S. Department of the Treasury. It facilitates impact investment in the projects.

The European Commission released an action plan for financing sustainable growth In March 2018. This plan included proposals for the regulation of disclosures on sustainable investment and sustainability risks. At the same time, GIIN published *The Roadmap for the Future of Impact Investing: Reshaping Financial Markets*. This report presents a vision for more inclusive and sustainable financial markets and articulates a plan for impact investment to lead progress toward this future (Bouri et al. 2018).

In February 2019, the U.S. Secretary of Commerce announced that 40 organizations, including nonprofits, institutions of higher education, and entrepreneurship-focused organizations, from 28 states and two territories will receive $21 million to create and expand cluster-focused entrepreneurship and technology transfer programs, and early-stage seed fund support under EDA's 2018 Regional Innovation Strategies (RIS) program competition. This can be viewed as an impact investment in the field of entrepreneurship, technology, and innovation.

The World Bank Group launched the Operating Principles for Impact Management at Spring Meetings in Washington, District of Columbia in April 2019. The Impact Principles provide a framework for investors to ensure that impact considerations are purposefully integrated throughout the investment life cycle. The initiative to develop these principles was led by International Finance Corporation (IFC), with the purpose of fostering increased mobilization of capital for impact. By December 2019, the financial flows into the U.S. sustainable funds topped $20 billion, which was more than quadruple the previous annual record for net flows for sustainable funds set in 2018 according to Liu.

At the end of 2019, the coronavirus pandemic spread around the world. It posed unprecedented challenges to every industry and sector, including the non-profit and social enterprise sector in China and around the globe. For example, a survey conducted by the Capacity Building Assessment Center (CBAC) in China shows that 89% of non-profit organizations in China are experiencing a lack of operating funds and shutdowns (Gu 2019). Similarly, a recent study by the Charities Aid Foundation of America shows that 73% of nonprofits have clearly felt a sharp decline in fundraising revenue.

Despite the grand challenge, many organizations and impact investors took initiatives to respond to the crisis. For example, in March 2020, the NYC COVID-19 Response and Impact Fund was created to aid non-profit service providers. The Rockefeller Foundation committed $20 million to create a better tracking and management system for COVID-19. Blackrock announced $50 million to help meet the immediate needs of those most affected. The World Bank and IFC jointly approved a package of $14 billion to strengthen national systems to strengthen the national system for public health preparedness (including disease diagnostics and treatment) and to support the private sector.

In April 2020, Big Society Capital launched a £100 million program of loans, including a new Resilience and Recovery Loan Fund. The Omidyar Network India announced rapid response funding to support lower income groups dealing with COVID-19. The Inter-American Development Bank (IDB) issued a sustainable development bond of $2 billion to support vulnerable populations. GIIN launched the Product Development Platform and hosted three successive Product Structure Workshops in the subsequent months. The workshops are intended to shed light on investment requirements for products that specifically respond to COVID-19 and to provide the managers structuring those products with feedback.

The Response, Recovery, and Resilience Investment Coalition (R3 Coalition) was launched by GIIN in May 2020. It is an industry initiative that aims to highlight impact investing opportunities and mobilize and coordinate impact investors to address the social and economic consequences of COVID-19. In the months that followed, the R3 Coalition released four successive Issue Briefs. The first issue brief provides an overview of the current state of play for impact investors. The second outlines strategies that address due diligence constraints. The third describes the common challenges faced by enterprises and investors' support for them during the time of the crisis. The final brief investigates the role of social equality in bringing a future that is resilient to crisis.

Later in May, Acumen, Center for Disease Control and Prevention (CDC), Responsibility Investments AG, and Shell Foundation jointly established the Covid-19 Energy Access Relief Fund to address concerns about the impact of COVID-19 on enterprises providing energy products and services to customers in Sub-Saharan Africa and Asia. The Bank of America announced the issuance of a $1 billion corporate social bond, the first such offering by a U.S. commercial bank. In June 2020, Ford Foundation announced a plan to offer $1 billion of social bonds for sale to fund an anti-Covid19 program—it is "the first non-profit foundation in history to offer a labeled social bond in the US taxable corporate bond market".

In October 2021, the EU set up the world's largest green bond in 15 years, raising €12 billion for green and sustainable investments in 27 EU member states. It is mainly used by EU member states to popularize renewable energy and improve energy efficiency. In addition, in the same year, the impact investments of the Rise Fund of TPG continued to expand, with the fund's total assets under management exceeding $5 billion by 2021.

2 The Current Trends of Impact Investing

2.1 Scales and Current Trend

The latest statistics on impact investments are provided in two GIIN reports: (1) *The State of Impact Measurement and Management Practice*, and (2) *Sizing the Impact Investing Market*. *The State of Impact Measurement and Management Practice* is based on 278 impact investing organizations that had (a) committed at least $10 million in impact investment since inception, or (b) actively measured the social and/or environmental performance of their investment (Mudaliar et al. 2017). Therefore, the statistics in this report reflect the scale of a sample of impact investors rather than the overall scale of the impact investing market. As of September 2019, 275 respondents managed $246 billion in impact investing assets. On average, each respondent managed $895 million, whereas the median respondent managed $80 million, given that several organizations managed large amounts of capital (Mudaliar et al. 2017).

The report *Sizing the Impact Investing Market* provides an estimation of the size of the impact investing market-based on a database of 1340 impact investing organizations. The size is estimated based on the impact investing AUM information for over 750 organizations (Mudaliar and Dithrich 2019). According to this report, the market size of impact investing is over 1340 organizations that currently manage $502 billion in impact investing assets worldwide as of the end of 2018 (Mudaliar and Dithrich 2019). On average, each respondent managed $452 million, whereas the median respondent managed $29 million (Mudaliar and Dithrich 2019). According to the Big Society Capital, the impact investment market in the United Kingdom was estimated to worth over £3.5 billion in 2019.

Impact investment has been growing rapidly, with new investors continuing to enter the market and contribute additional capital to create a positive impact (Mudaliar and Dithrich 2019). It demonstrates the growing trend based on the estimation indicated in GIIN's annual impact investor survey. We can find from Fig. 1 that, between 2015 and 2018, the number of impact investments has doubled, and the total capital invested increased by nearly 150%.

The growing trend is also demonstrated in an estimation from Morningstar (see Fig. 2). The net flows into ESG or sustainable funds available to the U.S. investors were $17.7 billion between January and November 2019, more than triple the record of the entire year 2018.

In 2015, the United Nations estimated that it would cost between $50 trillion and $70 trillion to achieve the Sustainable Development Goals (SDGs). As a response, the Rockefeller Foundation called for initiatives in leveraging innovative finance and tapping into private capital of more than $200 trillion to help implement the SDGs (Madsbjerg and Keohane 2016). The World Investment Report published by the United Nations Conference and Trade and Development in 2014 provides a bold framework to enhance the role of the private sector contributions to the SDG goals. To meet the SDGs, according to the report, $3.9 trillion annual investment is needed to fill in the $2.5 trillion annual funding gap (UNCTAD 2014). See Fig. 3.

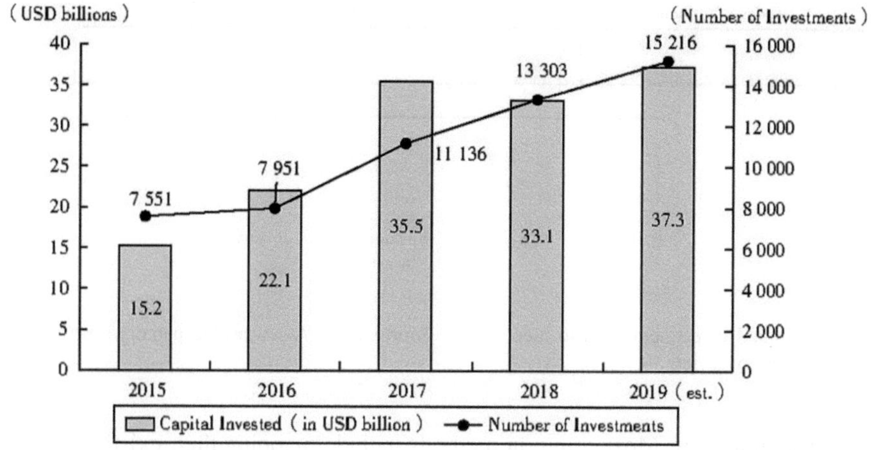

Fig. 1 The growing trends of impact investment (2015–2019). *Source* GIIN, GIIN Annual Impact Investor Survey, 2015–2019

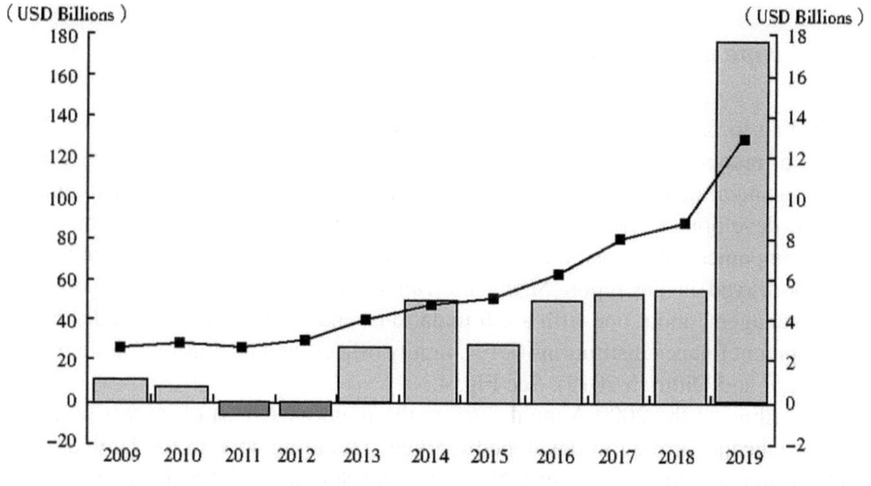

Fig. 2 Annual estimated ESG flows. *Source* Morningstar Direct. Data as of 11/2019. Includes ESG Integration, Impact, and Sustainable Sector funds as defined in Sustainable Funds U.S. Landscape Report, 2018. Includes funds that have been liquidated; does not include funds of funds

As indicated in the GIIN Annual Impact Surveys, impact investors have been actively tracking the performance of their investments to the SDG goals. They reported tracking the SDGs for a variety of reasons, with the greatest share of respondents (90%) indicating that they do so in order to communicate their impact externally or to integrate into the global development paradigm (Mudaliar et al. 2019). There are multiple ways through which impact investors incorporate the SDGs into their

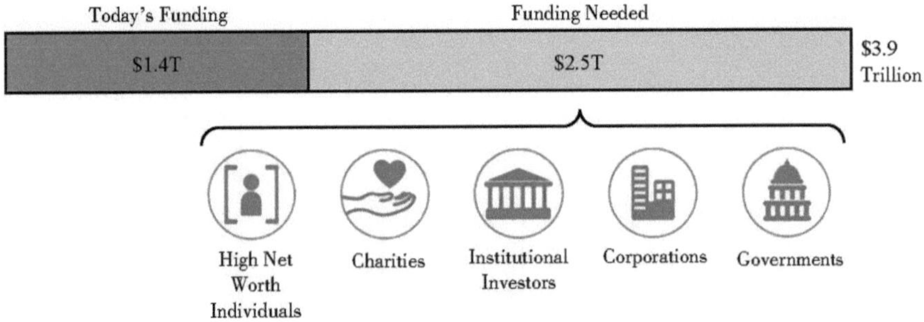

Fig. 3 Annual investment need to meet SDGs. *Source* https://www.bridgespan.org/services/impact-investing-overview

investing practices. Most common methods include mapping their existing portfolios to the SDGs and incorporating the SDGs into their impact measurement and management systems (Mudaliar et al. 2019).

2.2 *Scope and Distribution*

According to *State of Impact Measurement and Management Practice*, two-thirds (67%) of respondents identify as fund managers, while the remaining are various other organization types, including foundations, banks or diversified financial institutions, development finance institutions (DFI), family offices, permanent investment companies, and pension funds (Mudaliar et al. 2019). The breakdown is similarly portrayed in the report *Sizing the Impact Investing Market*: Over 60% are asset managers, about one-fifth are foundations, and the remaining includes banks, development finance institutions (DFI), family offices, and institutional asset owners (Mudaliar and Dithrich 2019). See Fig. 4.

According to the 2020 Annual Survey, the majority (77%) of impact organizations are headquartered in developed markets, including 45% in the United States and Canada and 26% in Western, Northern, and Southern (WNS) Europe. 21% are based in emerging markets, including 7% in Sub-Saharan Africa (SSA), 6% in Latin America and the Caribbean, and 11% in Asia. Figure 5 demonstrates the breakdown. Over the past four years, growth has been fastest in Western, Northern, and Southern Europe and East and Southeast Asia, at a rate of 25% and 23%, respectively.

Over one-third of the invested capital and nearly 70% of transactions were invested through private debt. Over the past four years and among repeated survey respondents, allocations through public equity and real assets have grown fastest, at 33% and 21%, respectively.

According to the GIIN 2020 Annual Survey, respondents have allocated the greatest share of assets to energy (15%), microfinance (13%), and other financial

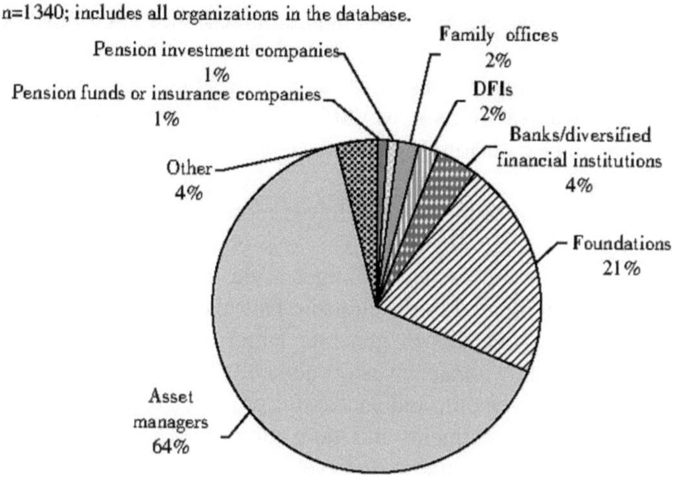

Fig. 4 Organizations by type. *Note* "Other" includes corporations, community development finance institutions, and non-governmental organizations. *Source* GIIN, Sizing the Impact Investing Market

Fig. 5 Headquarter location of impact investment agencies. *Source* GIIN 2020 Annual Survey

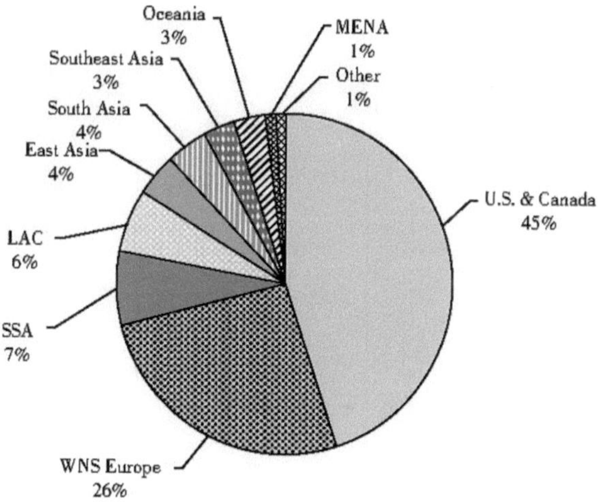

services (11%). From 2015 to 2019, repeated respondents grew their capital allocations most quickly to water, sanitation, and hygiene (WASH), at a rate of 33%, and to financial services (excluding microfinance) at a rate of 30%.

The report *State of Impact Measurement and Management Practice* specifics the distribution of impact investors targeting impact categories (Mudaliar et al. 2017). The greatest share of impact investors (71%) aim to generate employment, and nearly two-thirds focus on agriculture (63%) or financial services (62%). Respondents also demonstrate a strong commitment to providing other basic services, such as health

(60%), education (56%), energy (56%), and climate issues (54%) (Mudaliar et al. 2017).

The distribution of impact investment can also be summarized in terms of development stages. Impact investors serve different organizations in four stages: seed, start-up, growth, and expansion. Figure 6 lists some leading impact investors in the four different stages.

In the past years, impact investment flowed increasingly from the United States and Europe to global south countries. This is probably because of three reasons. Firstly, global south countries have a larger scale and scope of social problems and social demands compared to developed countries. They are thus larger "social markets." Impact investments can generate larger social impact in large social markets. Secondly, leading impact investors generally have the goal of making impact investment a global movement, and successful practices in global south countries would encourage more investments and more attention. Thirdly, the flow of impact investments from developed countries to developing countries can be viewed as a new type of globalization, following economic globalization. That is the globalization of impact investments.

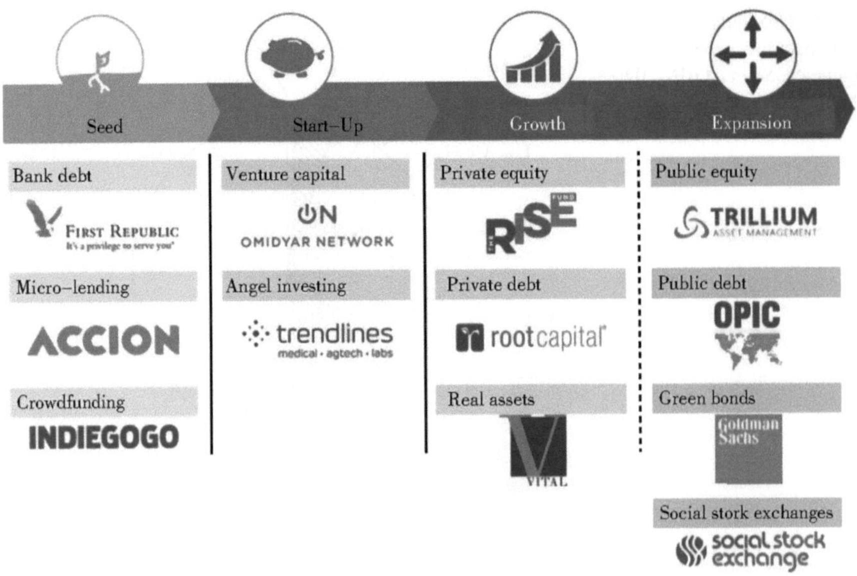

Fig. 6 Four stages of impact investment. *Note* The majority of capital sources at the seed and start-up phases are impact agnostic. *Source* https://www.bridgespan.org/services/impact-investing-overview

3 Measurement and Evaluation of Impact Investing

3.1 Principle and Criteria

Measurement and evaluation of Impact Investment is a particular type of evaluation that "seeks to answer a specific cause-and-effect question: What is the impact (or causal effect) of a program on an outcome of interest?" (Gertler et al. 2016). Social impact evaluations measure "treatment effects, for which treatment means being exposed to an intervention, such as a new policy or project, and effects are the difference that exposure makes to outcomes, such as income, productivity, poverty, health, and many other aspects" (White and Raitzer 2018). Figure 7 demonstrates the general process of social impact generation and evaluation, from input and activities to output, outcome, and impact.

Impact investments have started looking increasingly into measuring and evaluating social impact in a quantitative way, with a growing number of investors taking the Sustainable Development Goals (SDGs) as a reference. On April 12, 2019, IFC—the commercial arm of the World Bank Group—released "Operating Principles for Impact Management." The proposed principles integrate impact considerations throughout the entire investment lifecycle (see Fig. 8).

Drawing insights from existing literature, the IFC report summarizes four levels of social impact from product and industry level to policy and value level. The report also specifies 12 indicators or metrics to measure the impact.

Level 1–Product or service level

- Providing more products or services
- Generating more revenue

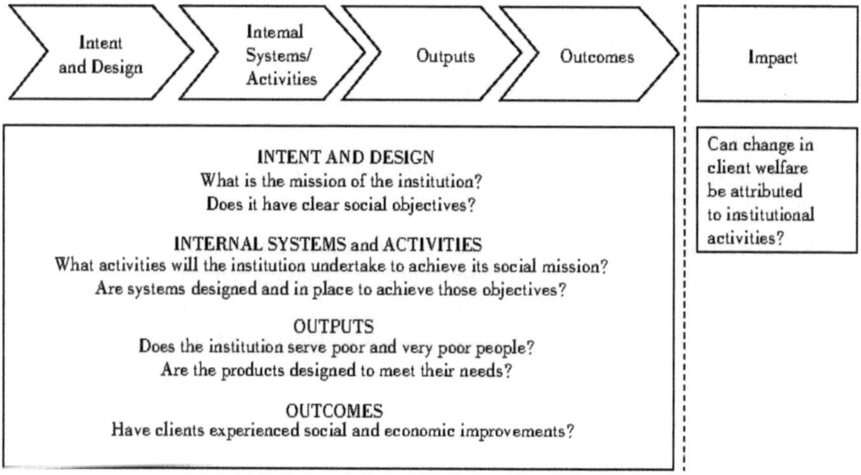

Fig. 7 General process of impact generation and evaluation. *Source* Gertler et al.

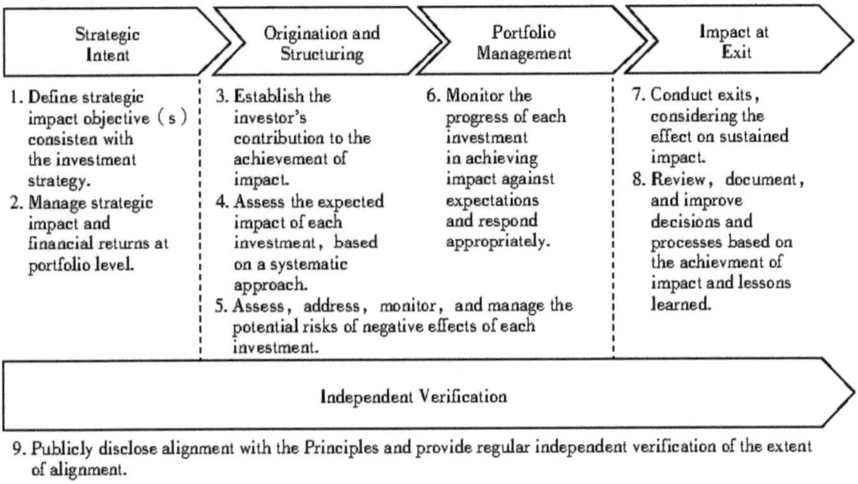

Fig. 8 Operating principles for impact management. *Source* World Bank Group. Operating Principles for Impact Management https://www.impactprinciples.org/principles

- Serving more people or more communities
- Expanding to wider geographic regions.

Level 2–Industry or market level

- Addressing a social problem or demand more effectively
- Creating a new industry, field, or market
- Establishing a social movement.

Level 3–Policy or legislation level

- Changing government policies
- Changing legislations or laws.

Level 4–Behavior, mindset, or value level

- Changing individual behaviors
- Changing public awareness or perception of an issue
- Changing values, norms, or cultures.

Most social impact evaluations usually look at indicators or metrics at level 1 or level 2, and seldom examine level 3 and level 4 of social impact. This report suggests that the future social impact evaluation should develop more sophisticated methods and instruments to measure and evaluate level 3 and level 4 of social impact.

3.2 Methods and Instruments

Although impact measurements and evaluations are at the early stage of development, several frequent methods and tools have emerged. The frequent methods and tools for measuring social impact include the following six types: (1) theory of change, (2) RCT (randomized controlled trial), (3) instrumental variable estimation, (4) regression discontinuity design, (5) difference in differences, and (6) propensity score matching (Gertler et al. 2016). Each impact evaluation method has its strengths and limitations, and the best method is the one that best aligns with the objective for measuring social impact in limited resources and conditions.

- Theory of change

The theory of change describes through a causal logic how an intervention, program, or organization delivers the desired results and impact. It depicts a sequence of events or a pathway: input-activities-outputs-outcomes-impact. A theory of change can be developed at the beginning of a project or intervention or to describe, analyze, or evaluate an existing piece of work, by involving a variety of stakeholders, including staff, trustees, beneficiaries, partners, and investors.

- RCT (Randomized Controlled Trial)

RCT is one of the most rigorous methods to measure social impact. It is a design that randomly assigns participants, programs, or organizations into an experimental group or a control group. When the process is completed, the only expected difference between the control and experimental group in a randomized controlled trial (RCT) is the outcome or impact of our focus. RCT is often used in impact evaluation in international development.

- Instrumental variable estimation

The method of instrumental variables (IV) is to estimate causal relationships when controlled experiments are not feasible or when a treatment is not successfully delivered to every unit in a randomized experiment. A valid instrument induces changes in the explanatory variable but has no independent effect on the dependent variable, allowing a researcher to uncover the causal effect of the explanatory variable on the dependent variable.

- Regression Discontinuity Design

Regression discontinuity design (RDD) is a quasi-experimental pretest–posttest design that elicits the causal effects of interventions by assigning a cutoff or threshold above or below which an intervention is assigned. By comparing observations lying closely on either side of the threshold, it is possible to estimate the average treatment effect in environments in which randomization is unfeasible.

- Difference in Differences

Difference in differences can measure the differential effect of a treatment on a "treatment group" versus a "control group" in a natural experiment. It calculates the effect of a treatment (i.e., an independent variable) on an outcome (i.e., a dependent variable) by comparing the average change over time in the outcome variable for the treatment group, compared to the average change over time for the control group.

- Propensity Score Matching

Propensity score matching (PSM) is a statistical matching technique that attempts to estimate the effect of a treatment, policy, or other intervention by accounting for the covariates that predict receiving the treatment. PSM aims to reduce the bias due to confounding variables that could be found in an estimate of the treatment effect obtained from simply comparing outcomes among units that received the treatment versus those that did not.

To sum up, the theory of change is frequently adopted by nonprofits, social enterprises, and impact investors in impact evaluation and business planning. RCT is an experimental design of measuring social impact, which is the most rigorous but expensive. The other methods are more advanced and require high-quality quantitative data that are often not available. In many cases, impact investors and researchers also use qualitative methods to describe or evaluate impacts, such as interviews, case studies, and even storytelling.

The six types of social impact evaluation methods are the mainstream and most frequently used ones, especially in the era prior to big data. In the time of big data and cloud technology, more innovative, real-time, online, and cost-effective methods are emerging. For example, a Silicon Valley startup developed an impact cloud, namely "SoPact." SoPact is an online platform that "allows funders, mission-driven organizations, and sustainable organizations to easily measure and manage their social and environmental impact." SoPact represents the future development of online social impact evaluation platforms. In the future, more advanced impact evaluation instruments are expected to emerge.

4 Policy and Legal Frameworks of Impact Investing

4.1 Legal Framework

The Insight at Pacific Community Ventures and the Initiative for Responsible Investment at Harvard University provides a policy and legal framework for impact investment, as demonstrated in Fig. 9 (Thornley et al. 2011). This framework has three sections: supply side, demand side, and the market in between. The supply side includes "providers of capital, including governments, individuals, foundations, banks, investment, and retirement funds" (Thornley et al. 2011). The demand side includes "the companies, cooperatives, projects, and other vehicles in need of capital" (Thornley et al. 2011). The market in between is the place where exchange occurs,

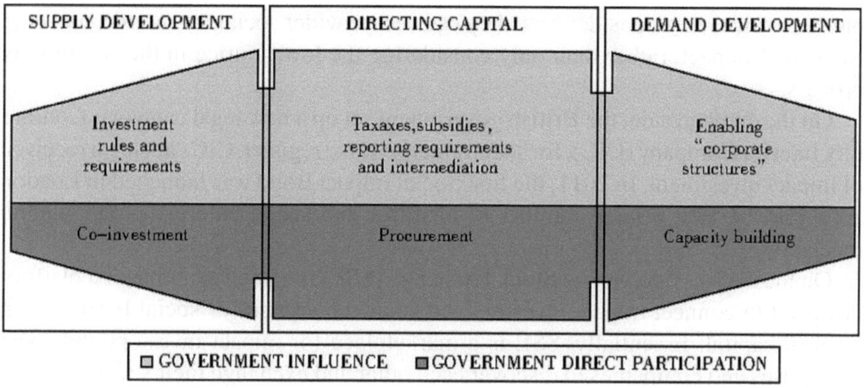

Fig. 9 Policy and legal framework for impact investment. *Source* Thornley et al. (2011)

"where rules govern the terms of trade and buyers and sellers set prices" (Thornley et al. 2011).

All policies and legal measures can be understood as working in three parts. On the supply side, for example, there is an increasing amount of capital for investment (supply development). On the demand side, there is an increasing availability or strengthening of the capacity of capital recipients (demand development). On the market side: Adjusting policies or regulations on trade, market norms, or prices (directing capital)" (Thornley et al. 2011).

Through these three aspects, the government can participate directly in impact investment or influence the sector indirectly. The following section reviews the United Kingdom and the United States as examples and illustrates their policy and legal framework for impact investment.

4.2 *United Kingdom*

The United Kingdom witnessed the first series of pioneering practices in impact investment as well as a range of supportive policies by the British government in the past two decades (Han et al. 2020). This report uses the framework to analyze the policies and players in the impact investment industry of the United Kingdom, from the three aspects of supply, demand, and market.

On the supply side, for example, UnLtd, the largest social enterprise supporting network in the United Kingdom, was founded as early as 2002 by an endowment from the Millennium Commission to conduct impact investment. In 2009, the U.K. Department of Health launched the Social Enterprise Investment Fund (SEIF) to support social enterprises in delivering health and social care services. In 2012, Big Society Capital was launched (Han 2017b). In 2013, the Public Services Act or Social Value Act came into force. The Act requires public sector agencies that commission public services to reconsider how they can secure wider social, economic, and environmental impact, rather than only considering the lowest price in the commission process.

On the demand side, the British government set up a new legal category, Community Interest Company (CIC), for social enterprises to register. CICs are legal receivers of impact investment. In 2011, the first Social Impact Bond was launched in London. As a part of SIB, a large number of charities and social enterprises are funding receivers.

On the market side, Social Stock Exchange (SSE) is a good example of a platform designed to connect impact investors and social enterprises or social businesses in need of capital. Essentially, SSE is a marketplace for impact investors and social enterprises and companies to discover each other and exchange their social stocks or equities. SSE set up a directory of companies that passed "social impact tests," and the businesses on the list can get better visibility from impact investors (Chhichhia 2015). Two other prominent policies implemented in the United Kingdom are the Community Investment Tax Relief (CITR) in 2012 and Social Investment Tax Relief (SITR) in 2014. The CITR encourages investment in disadvantaged communities by giving tax relief to investors who invested in community organizations. SITR encourages individuals to invest in social enterprises, charities, and community businesses by receiving a 30% tax break on SITR investments.

4.3 United States

Similar to the United Kingdom, the United States has also introduced a series of legal and policy measures to support impact investment. Similarly, these legal and policy measures can be analyzed in three dimensions: the supply side, the demand side, and the market side.

On the supply side, one of the early policies is the issue of the *Community Reinvestment Act* in 1977, which prohibited lending practices that discriminate against low-income communities. Some of the other widely acknowledged early laws to support impact investment include the launch of the U.S. Sustainable Investment Forum (US SIF) in 1984, the Community Development Financial Institutions (CDFIs) Act of 1994, and the establishment of the Community Development Financial Institutions Fund by the U.S. Treasury in 1994 (Lumberg 2017; Nicholls et al. 2015). In 2009, the Obama Administration opened the Office of Social Innovation and Civic Participation. The office afterward created the Social Innovation Fund and partnered with philanthropic founders including private foundations, community foundations, corporations, and individual donors to sponsor the development of impact investment (Toepler 2018a).

On the demand side, social enterprises can register as low-profit limited liability companies (L3C) and benefit corporations in the United States to receive impact investment. L3C was primarily designed to facilitate program-related investments from philanthropic foundations to social enterprises without charitable non-profit status (Schmidt 2010; Chan 2011). In 2008, Vermont was the first state to establish the L3C as an official legal structure for social enterprises. By 2018, eight states in the United States recognized low L3C as an official legal status, and three states were considering doing so. Benefit corporation is designed to anchor the pursuit of social benefit in the corporate charter (Toepler 2018b). In 2010, Maryland passed the first benefit corporation legislation. According to the Social Enterprise Law Tracker developed by New York University, thirty-four states in the United States have enacted the Benefit Corporation legislation as of April 2019, and eight states are now considering passing the legislation.

On the market side, the United States has a unique legal framework for impact investments in underdeveloped communities called Opportunity Zone. Opportunity Zones are economically disadvantaged communities that have been officially designated by states and then certified at a federal level so that private investment in these areas can be made eligible for special tax treatment. The purpose of Opportunity Zones, which were introduced in 2017 as part of the Tax Cuts and Jobs Act, is to catalyze the use of private capital (instead of taxpayer funds) to stimulate growth in these traditionally marginalized communities. Opportunity Zones provide three main tax benefits for investing through a qualified Opportunity Fund: (1) a temporary deferral of inclusion in taxable income for capital gains reinvested; (2) a step-up in basis for capital gains reinvested, and (3) a permanent exclusion from taxable income of capital gains from the sale or exchange of an investment in an Opportunity Fund if the investment is held for at least ten years. These benefits of Opportunity Zones have captured the attention of funders, investors, asset managers, policymakers, and community development financial institutions. As of year-end 2018, there are more than 8700 Opportunity Zones officially designated, representing 12% of the census tracts in the United States. The Economic Innovation Group provides maps that show the detailed activities within each Opportunity Zone, including the name of the Opportunity fund and the functionality of the investment.

4.4 Policy Support for Social Enterprises

Social enterprises are often receivers of impact investments. From the perspective of value chains or supply chains, impact investors are in the upstream, while social enterprises are in the downstream. The collaborations between impact investors and social enterprises create social impact. To promote impact investments, it is important and necessary to understand the policy frameworks for social enterprise so that impact investors can make more informed, purposeful, and targeted investment decisions.

Governments around the world have been providing policy support for the social enterprise sector through a variety of measures and agendas. The modes and degrees of governmental support to the social enterprise sector differ by three main aspects: (1) governmental recognition of social enterprises as reflected in their presence in official documents; (2) governmental support in the short and long terms through direct or indirect means; (3) governmental facilitation of social enterprise programs by coordinating with enabling agencies (Agapitova et al. 2017).

The level of government engagement differs by country. Countries such as the United States, the United Kingdom, and South Korea are characterized by a mature policy framework. In these countries, Governments recognize the importance of social enterprises as part of their national plans, laws, and strategies. There are comprehensive policy tools to support different stages of growth of social enterprises, including resources for early-stage development and suggestions for capacity building. The second group of countries includes Canada, Chile, Italy, Malaysia, Poland, and Thailand. These countries see growing governmental support for legalizing and expanding the social enterprise sector. Social enterprises and supporting agencies in these countries have formed networks that are likely to expand. In some other countries, such as Columbia, Egypt, and India, policies in support of social enterprises are at an emerging stage and are usually included as part of a broader agenda. For example, the Ministry of Skills Development and Entrepreneurship in India has adopted the Enterprise Policy, which includes a section on social entrepreneurship that provides a definition for the term and outlines specific forms of support. Finally, in countries where policies supporting social enterprises are in early stages, such as Kenya and South Africa, social enterprises are not recognized under formal legal form, and they benefit mostly from programs that facilitate NGOs or small and medium-sized enterprises (Agapitova et al. 2017).

Similar to the four stages of policy support to social enterprises, the policy and legal framework for impact investment can consider the four stages (early, emerging, growing, and mature) too. Overall, impact investments in the United Kingdom and the United States are at the emerging stage. China is at an early stage. There is still a long way to go, both for the two leading countries and for China and the rest of the world. This report recommends practitioners and scholars of impact investment take a close look at the legal and policy frameworks of impact investments in the United Kingdom and the United States, as well as the global policy framework of social enterprises, in order to better develop impact investments.

5 Challenges of the Global Impact Investing

A major challenge of impact investing is balancing and delivering an appropriate financial return to investors while maximizing positive social impact to communities (or addressing the issue the investors are attempting to resolve). According to Durreen Shahnaz, founder and CEO of the Impact Investment Exchange (IIX) in Singapore, investors are averse to taking risks with impact investing. She recalled her experience with IIX's Women's Livelihood Bond in 2016 to share that impact investing, indeed, comes with its own set of risks. However, as Shahnaz mentions, "they are supposed to be complicated because you're trying to solve very complex social issues and environmental issues".

Impact investments often have difficulties consistently measuring across different investments due to the vast array of results and a lack of commonality. There are also challenges in quantifying and comparing impact (impact measurement) as well as management practice of each investment. In the report "Impact investment: The Challenge and Opportunity of Social Impact Bonds," the Young Foundation highlights the importance of a robust measurement system that has no systematic bias.

As listed in the GIIN Survey, other challenges of impact investments include: the lack of government support for the impact investment market, the lack of professionals with relevant skill sets, suitable exit options, and the lack of common understanding of definition of segmentation of the impact investing market (Mudaliar et al. 2019).

According to the survey respondents, a lack of "appropriate capital across the risk/return spectrum" is the most significant challenge (41%) facing impact investors. Over a third of the survey respondents noted a lack of "suitable exit options," limited "sophistication of impact measurement and management practice," and a lack of "high-quality investment opportunities with track records" as other significant challenges. Meanwhile, only about one in five respondents identified the availability of "professionals with relevant skill sets" and "research on market activities, trends, performance, and practice" as significant challenges (Mudaliar et al. 2019).

For emerging economies, there are even more challenges to the development of impact investments. Firstly, the awareness of the importance and the operation of impact investments is lacking or weak in emerging economies. For emerging economies, economic development or GDP growth is often the top priority. Social problems and social demands have not attracted sufficient attention. Taking advantage of the power of finance to innovatively address social problems and meet social demands has not been placed clearly in their economic or policy agendas.

Secondly, investor communities in emerging economies are at the emerging or growing stage too. The maximization of the financial return is still the top concern. Generating both financial return and social impact demands the maturity and prosperity of the investor communities. According to the Stanford Social Innovation Review, while there are 44 current impact bonds in existence and approximately 100 under development in various developed countries, only one impact bond has been initiated domestically in developing countries. Developing countries have to address the challenges of the complexity of impact investment, strict data and measurement requirements, and the availability of sufficient private funding sources.

Thirdly, in developing countries, neither input costs nor outcome data are readily available. The lack of data and transparency makes it harder for investors to understand which companies are sustainable and whether investments are impactful. Without stable, accurate, and unbiased data, sustainable investment decisions would be difficult. The World Economic Forum further strengthens that argument, "where disclosure and data exist, there tend to be record levels of sustainable investing".

6 The Future of Impact Investing Globally

GIIN has mapped out the roadmap for the future development of social impact investing in terms of six categories: (1) strengthening the identity of impact investing by establishing clear principles and standards for practice, (2) reshaping investors behavior and expectations through aligning incentives with impact (3) expanding impact investment products to serve a full spectrum of investors, (4) developing tools and services to support the integration of impact into investors' routine analysis, allocation, and deal-making activities, (5) bolstering education and training to increase awareness of impact investing and maintain the integrity of practice, and (6) enhancing policy and regulation to create an environment conducive to impact investing (Bouri et al. 2018).

This book highlights five points for the future trend of impact investment. Firstly, the scale and scope of impact investments will continue to expand. According to GIIN 2019 Annual Survey, the impact investment market has already reached US$500 billion at the end of 2018 (Mudaliar et al. 2019). The upper end of market estimates predicts impact investing to reach as much as $1 trillion by 2020 (O'donohoe et al. 2010). The Survey also finds that impact actors are committed to further development of the impact investing industry, with over 80% making some contribution toward the various actions recommended in GIIN's Roadmap for Future of Impact investing. That includes sharing best practices for impact measurement and management, supporting the development of businesses focused on impact, and training finance professionals (Mudaliar et al. 2019). Additionally, there is wide acknowledgment of progress on major indicators of market growth, such as research on market activity, availability of professionals with relevant skill sets, and government support for the market. Given the growing trends and the growing interest, the impact investment industry is expected to continue expanding and evolving.

Secondly, the ecosystem of impact investments will become mature in the next 10–20 years. Institutional organizations, intermediary organizations, and support organizations for impact investment agencies will become more diverse and professional. Leading impact investment agencies will continue to emerge and grow. Impact actors are committed to providing leadership and expertise to support shared learning experiences and to collaborating with other actors to nurture an ecosystem that is robust, aligned, highly qualified, and ethical (Council of Michigan Foundations 2013).

Thirdly, the supporting policies for impact investments will expand locally and spread globally. Governments around the world will demonstrate greater commitments to expand impact investment. Over the past few years, the United States designated the first set of Opportunity Zones, France launched the French Impact Initiative, Portugal approved the creation of Fund for Social Innovation (FIS), and G20 Leaders recognized impact investment as a driver of inclusive and sustainable business (Mudaliar et al. 2019). According to the Roadmap, most impact actors believe that governments can catalyze industry growth to a greater extent in the future than they have thus far (Bouri et al. 2018). The governments are expected to adopt policies that help increase transparency or create demand for more investment opportunities with a positive impact. Provision of credit enhancement and funding capacity-building support for investees are also widely seen as useful roles that governments will adopt.

Fourthly, the ongoing Fourth Industrial Revolution is changing the impact investment significantly. According to the Roadmap highlighted by GIIN, the Fourth Industrial Revolution is probably shaping the future of impact investing in four aspects (Bouri et al. 2018). (1) The increasing automation of work requires that impact investors adapt their strategies to support their target beneficiaries through the changes, perhaps by investing in skills development or in sectors where jobs are less susceptible to obsolescence (Bouri et al. 2018). (2) The emergence of Fintech affects investor preferences and modes of operating, generating unprecedented opportunities for product developers to take advantage of the efficiency benefits of technology to channel more capital into socially and environmentally positive investments (Bouri et al. 2018). (3) The gig data and blockchain technology will bring impact investment the accountability, transparency, and movement it has needed to sustain its upward trend in market performance and presence (Bouri et al. 2018). These are examples of how megatrends related to technological changes and shifts in client preferences may affect the industry of impact investment.

Fifthly, in the global spread of the Covid-19 pandemic, the world has witnessed renewed calls for impact investments as an immediate response to the global fight against the epidemic. During the gradual recovery of the international public healthcare system and the restoration of faith in distributive justice and global governance, investment with social welfare and responsibility as its goal is playing an increasingly important role across the bonds between public and private spheres and the boundaries between nation-states. As Amit Bouri, CEO and Co-Founder of the GIIN, highlights, leveraging robust and scalable financial investments is key to addressing global challenges like the COVID-19 pandemic. Although in the difficult time of COVID-19, impact investors have remained committed to their previous investing plans. They continue to contribute, growing the market from $502 billion in 2019 to $715 billion this year.

The past few months have also witnessed significant growth in social bonds, signifying the appeal and endurance of social bonds as a sustainable finance instrument in combating crises (Gu 2019). Future sustainable solutions to the world's major crises will continue relying on the informed and inspired choices of investors.

References

Agapitova N, Sanchez B, Tinsley E (2017) Government support to the social enterprise sector. The World Bank

Bouri A et al (2018) Roadmap for the future of impact investing: reshaping financial markets. GIIN. https://thegiin.org/research/publication/giin-roadmap

Chan E (2011) The L3C–3 years later. Nonprofit law blog. http://www.nonprofitlawblog.com/the-l3c-3-years-later/

Chhichhia B (2015) The rise of social stock exchanges: a new, innovative platform is helping more investors support social enterprises. Stanford social innovation review. https://ssir.org/articles/entry/the_rise_of_social_stock_exchanges

Council of Michigan Foundations (2013) Strategic planning task force: roles and responsibilities. https://www.michiganfoundations.org/sites/default/files/CMF%20Impact%20Investing%20Ecosystem%20Development%20%281%29.pdf

Gertler PJ et al (2016) Impact evaluation in practice, 2nd ed. World Bank and Inter-American Development Bank

Gu L (2019) Interviewed by Rae Winborn. CASVI Interview

Han J, Chen W, Toepler S (2020) Social finance for nonprofits: impact investing, social impact bonds, and crowdfunding. The Routledge Companion to Nonprofit Management

Han J (2017b) Social marketisation and policy influence of third sector organisations: evidence from the UK, VOLUNTAS: Int J Volunt Nonprofit Organ 28:1209–1225

Lumberg J (2017) A history of impact investing. Investopedia. https://www.investopedia.com/news/history-impact-investing/

Madsbjerg S, Keohane GL (2016) The innovative finance revolution: private capital for the public good. Foreign Aff 95

Mudaliar A, Dithrich H (2019) Sizing the impact investing market. The GIIN. https://thegiin.org/research/publication/impinv-market-size. Accessed 31 July 2019

Mudaliar A et al (2017) The state of impact measurement and management practice. https://thegiin.org/research/publication/imm-survey

Mudaliar A et al (2019) Annual impact investor survey. GIIN. https://thegiin.org/research/publication/impinv-survey-2019

Nicholls A, Paton R, Emerson J (eds) (2015) Social finance. Oxford University Press, Oxford

O'donohoe N et al (2010) Impact investments: an emerging asset class. J.P. Morgan, Rockefeller Foundation, GIIN. https://thegiin.org/research/publication/impact-investments-an-emerging-asset-class

Olson J, Phillips A (2013) Rikers Island: the first social impact bond in the United States. Community Development Investment Review, pp 97–101

Schmidt E (2010) Vermont's social hybrid pioneers: early observation and questions to ponder. Vermont Law Rev 35(1):163–209

Thornley B, Wood D, Grace K, Sullivant S (2011) Impact investing: a framework for policy design and analysis. Pacific community ventures. Initiative for Responsible Investment at Harvard University. The Rockefeller Foundation. http://www.pacificcommunityventures.org/wp-content/uploads/sites/6/2015/07/Impact_Investing_Policy_Full_Report.pdf

Toepler S (2018a) Do benefit corporations represent a policy threat to nonprofits? Nonprofit Policy Forum 9(4):1–9

Toepler S (2018b) Public philanthropic partnerships: the changing nature of government/foundation relationships in the US. Int J Public Adm 41(8):657–669

UNCTAD (2014) World investment report, p 140. https://worldinvestmentreport.unctad.org/wir2014/wir2014-ch4-promoting-private-sector-contributions

White H, Raitzer D (2018) Impact evaluation of development interventions: a practical guide. Asian Development Bank. https://www.adb.org/publications/impact-evaluation-development-interventions-practical-guide

Impact Investing in China

There is no denying its recent popularity around the world. Compared to many countries in the world, China's impact investment ecosystem was just in its early stage. Impact investing in China is an important case study for the industry globally, in large part due to China's potential market size and current importance in the financial market, as well as the unique challenges facing China's impact investing ecosystem. In many respects, China is a market well-suited for impact investing. Faced with looming social and environmental issues, the government's national development plans have laid out ambitious and sweeping goals for society's development and the amelioration of its most pressing social problems. Impact investment by the private sector has the potential to fill the funding gap necessary to meet these objectives. Issues most prominent in the minds of China's leaders include a fast-aging population, environmental pollution and destruction, and increasing income inequality (especially in rural areas).

In addition to promising government mandates, the growth of China's traditional private investment industry continues to attract both international and local investor attention. Local investors are becoming more investment savvy and more socially aware. Adam Bendell, CEO of Toniic, the global impact investing organization for asset owners, claimed that China's "spirit of innovation and rising wealth" makes it a "natural hotspot for impact investing" (Bouton 2018).

On the other hand, many of the underlying assumptions and beliefs of key stakeholders in China are different than those in other countries. Globally, major governments and non-government stakeholders have bought into the premise of impact investing. Fundamentally, impact investing challenges the notion that only philanthropic institutions can address social and environmental issues, while financial institutions should exclusively focus on financial returns. In China, the roles of government, civil society, and the private sector are historically different than of those institutions in the West.

Despite China's market potential, little research has been conducted on this market and its evolution in recent years, especially in comparison to an increasingly diverse library of existing literature on global impact investing. Existing literature is limited

Finance Center for South-South Cooperation, *Impact Investing*,
https://doi.org/10.1007/978-981-99-4935-9_3

to industry reports that often lack a theoretical framework for their analysis. These are primarily written by impact investors or active promoters of impact investing, which, while not invalidating their conclusions, may indicate a difference.

In addition, many previous reports (AVPN 2019b) have emphasized impact investing as a philanthropic tool rather than as an investment opportunity. Thus, their reports focus on the potential social issues impact investing can address and the capital demands of the investee portfolio companies, rather than the opportunity of impact investing in and of itself. This perspective, while important for entities receiving capital, is not as useful for potential investors trying to understand the market opportunity of impact investing.

This chapter provides a comprehensive overview of the impact investing ecosystem in China, including its opportunities and challenges. Based on extensive interviews with market participants and supporters, as well as existing research and public data, this chapter examines six key factors of impact investing in China: market supply and demand, policy, finance, culture, support, and human capital.

In this chapter, it will be divided into four sections. Firstly, we will review the historical development of the impact investing in China in different stages. Secondly, we will discuss the development of the Chinese impact investing ecosystem and the current state of the market. Thirdly, we will analyze factors influencing the market using Rivera Acevedo and Wu's (2018) Impact Investing Ecosystem Framework. Fourthly, we will conclude with a summary of key findings and provide recommendations.

Our research highlights several important characteristics of China's impact investing ecosystem. Evidence indicates that China's impact investing ecosystem is still in its early stages of development. However, there has been a flurry of new international entrants and a significant wave of new interest in impact investing in recent years. Impact investors face similar challenges as global investors, including underdeveloped impact measurement systems and a lack of human capital resources. A narrative dominated by traditional philanthropy and a lack of collaboration and exchange with the international impact investing community are unique factors that distinguish China's impact investing market from other early-stage markets.

1 The Development of Impact Investing in China

Despite the nascent stage of China's impact investing ecosystem, impact investing is not new in China. While it is hard to pinpoint the exact timeframe when impact investing was introduced to China, Peking University-based journal *China Social Work Research* introduced the term "social enterprise" to Chinese academia in 2004 (Zhao 2012), and the first China Social Investment Forum took place in 2012. The history of impact investing in China can be roughly divided into four different stages.

1.1 Proto-Impact Investors (Pre-2007)

While impact investing was first defined in 2007, informal concepts of investing for social good had already existed in China's public and private sector. Government-guided funds (pools of capital financed by the central and local government or state-owned enterprises and used to invest in "strategic areas") have long been used to create social and economic impact. Social welfare enterprises, which employ disabled workers, are often considered "social enterprises with Chinese characteristics" (YouChange 2016). These entities are certified and regulated by the state, often receiving beneficial tax incentives.

There were also a few private funds leveraging early ideas of investing with social considerations. The earliest proto-impact investors include Beijing-based Tsing Capital, which raised its first China Environment Funds in 2002. Per Tsing Capital's website, it was "Founded in 2000 on the philosophy of 'Doing Well by Doing Good.'" However, it did not self-identify as an impact investor until more recently and was listed as an impact investor by Dao Ventures' 2012 report. Global private equity fund Small Enterprise Assistance Fund (SEAF) also established the USD 23 million SEAF Sichuan SME Investment Fund in 2001. These firms formally adopted an impact investing strategy later on. However, SEAF has not raised any follow-on funds for China, though it is still active globally. Tsing Capital is actively investing and currently manages two series of funds: the China Environment Funds and the Smart Innovation Funds.

1.2 The First Waves of Interest: Venture Philanthropists Lead the Way (2007–2010)

On the tail of the new international movement around impact investing, the first wave of venture philanthropists, many of which would either evolve to become impact investors or advocate for impact investing, surged around 2007. Similar to the Rockefeller Foundation's role in the global landscape, in China, impact investing was first advocated by foundations. YouChange and the Narada Foundation, two of the leading organizations supporting and advocating for impact investing in China today, were both founded in 2007. However, unlike global foundations, Chinese charitable organizations, including philanthropic foundations, are by definition unable to have a "profit-making purpose" (International Center for Not-for-Profit Law 2019). This may in part explain why venture philanthropy took off before impact investing.

LGT Venture Philanthropy was another early entrant to venture philanthropy in China. Founded in 2007, LGT Venture Philanthropy is the venture philanthropy arm of private banking and asset management firm LGT. LGT launched LGT Lightstone as its global impact investing initiative in 2019. While LGT continues to maintain its current investments and key relationships in China, due to the strong economic development and increased regulation in China, LGT Venture Philanthropy and Lighthouse decided to strategically focus its resources on Sub-Saharan Africa, Latin America, and India (Li 2019).

Several Hong Kong players that included mainland China in their remit also were established around this time, including Hong Kong-based SA Capital, which was founded in 2008. One of the earlier finance-first impact investors in Asia, they have made two investments in mainland China (Roque 2020). RS Group, a family office that is committed to investing across the social continuum of capital, was also established in 2008. Its impact investing strategy is global, and it typically invests as a limited partner (LP) into structured impact investment funds (RS Group 2016). RS Group has not made an impact investment in mainland China, either as a direct investment into a company or as an LP into a fund, but it does have several venture philanthropy projects in mainland China.

The British Council also started its Social Enterprise Programme in 2009. The program "trained over 3200 social entrepreneurs, facilitated RMB 37 million in social investment opportunities to 117 social enterprises and held salons, talks, and other public events which were attended by 17,000 actors from the social enterprise sector" (British Council 2016). The program closed in March 2016. Venture philanthropy fund Venture Avenue, which partnered with the British Council, was also founded in 2009 (Xu 2019). It is no longer investing, though it is still managing its existing portfolio.

1.3 The Second Wave: Financial-First Impact Investors Enter the Space (2010–2015)

In the first half of the 2010s, another wave of venture philanthropists and more profit-focused impact investors emerged in China. Venture philanthropists established during this wave include the foundation Leping Social Investment (which started as a microfinance organization and eventually branched into venture philanthropy) and the non-profit organization Yifang Foundation (which provides grants). Per our interviews with these organizations, impact investors established in this period include Dao Ventures, Lanshan Social Investment (no longer operating), Avantage Ventures (no longer operating), and Transist (rebranded as China Impact Ventures in 2016). Reflecting this new wave of interest, the Social Enterprise and Impact Investment Forum was also established in 2014.

1.4 The Third Wave: The Reentry of International Investors (Since 2015)

Since 2015, it has seen a steady trickle of new entrants. Traditional private equity firm UOB Venture Management raised their first Asia-focused impact investing fund, Asia

Impact Investment Fund, and subsequently invested in several China-based companies (FinNews Asia 2019). Previously mentioned China Impact Ventures was also founded in 2016 as a rebrand of Transist. China Impact Ventures closed its fund in 2018 and will no longer invest, though it is still managing its existing portfolio (Zheng 2019). NPI, a non-profit incubator founded in 2007, began making impact investments in 2016 from their NPI Social Venture Fund. They are currently reassessing their strategy and its sustainability (Li 2019). Impact Hub Shanghai, a network for impactful enterprises, was founded in 2017 and began incubating and funding social enterprises. It started an impact investing fund in 2019 (Lv 2019). Traditional private equity fund Ehong Capital states on its website that it has aimed to be a socially responsible investor since its founding in 2007, and established Ehe Impact Fund in 2018. Narada Foundation is a cornerstone LP.

Several global impact investors have entered or begun actively searching for investments. TPG Rise, the USD 2 billion global impact investing fund, made two investments in China, micro-loan companies Baidu Financial Services Group and China Foundation for Poverty Alleviation (CFPA) Microfinance Management in 2018 (TPG 2018). ABC World Asia has also raised an SGD 385 million fund with a geographic remit in China, Southeast Asia, and South Asia (ABC World Asia 2019). Smaller international and regional impact investing firms are also looking to invest in China, including 98 Sparks' PureTerra Fund and Mana Impact Partners, both of whom, were interviewed for this report.

There has been increased activity from global impact investors in China. In recent years, impact investors have been successful in raising larger, global, or regional funds (i.e., TPG Rise and ABC World Asia). China, as a large potential market, may start to look more attractive to larger players, especially if they are focusing on early-stage tech companies in impactful sectors such as healthcare or ed-tech. Of course, international impact investors of the first wave have all left the market, so it remains to see whether success will be achieved this time around.

2 The Current Impact Investing Ecosystem

2.1 Current State of Impact Investing Market in China

In recent years, more and more international investors have begun to pay attention to the Chinese market. As a senior executive of Dao Ventures, an impact investing firm in China, summarized in our interview, "Investors think there is a lot of money in China. There's a lot of talk about impact investing, but impact investors are few and far between, short on successful case studies, and work needs to be done on educating investors."

In 2008, only a couple of impact investors were active, such as Tsing Capital, SEAF, and SA Capital. So far, there have been a growing number of institutional impact investors operationally active in China.[1] Within the 11 impact investors which we mainly focus on, four of these impact investors were founded in China and three are international impact investors (98 Sparks, ABC World Asia, and Mana Impact Partners). Another four active international impact investors have made an investment (see Table 1).

Domestic impact investors' disclosed assets under management (AUM) ranged from USD 4.22 million (NPI) to USD 700 million (Tsing Capital), with the disclosed fund size ranging from USD 4.22 million (NPI) to USD 350 million (Tsing Capital). Funds backed by international LPs are much larger, given their remit extends beyond China, with TPG Rise's fund being the largest.

The majority of impact investors targeted early-stage venture investments. TPG Rise, UOB Venture Management, and ABC World Asia target growth investments. Most impact investors are targeting market-rate returns.

We traced around 34–81 impact investments from 2007 to 2020. The majority of investments have been small; of the nine investors disclosing average investment size, seven indicated that a typical investment was under USD 10 million. To put that in perspective, the average deal size for venture capital in China from 2015 to 1H 2019 was USD 29 million (EMPEA 2019).

In terms of investments, the most popular sectors targeted by impact investors are sustainable food/agriculture and the environment (including clean-tech, water solutions, and sustainable consumption, but not including large-scale renewable infrastructure). The most often cited opportunities for investment by interviewees (which include venture philanthropists) included healthcare (specifical eldercare), environment, and rural development and agriculture. Other noted investment areas include recycling and consumption, education, technology, and fin-tech.

While actual investment activity has not intensified, the amount of interest in impact investing has exploded. The China Global Philanthropy Institute organized the first Global Social Finance Forum and Social Impact Investing Summit (GSFF) in 2017, indicating enough demand and interest to organize a summit. Attendance at a similar conference, the China Social Enterprise and Impact Investment Forum, has increased from 500 participants in 2015 to over 1800 in 2021. The Triple Bottom Line Investing Group (TBLI Group), a conference, consulting, and advisory group for social finance, including impact investing and ESG, hosted its first TBLI Family Office Conference in Beijing in 2019. Anecdotally, interviewees have noted an increase in interest from high-net-worth individuals and family offices.

Given the growth in interest around impact investing globally and the number of impact funds raised by traditional investors like KKR, Bain Capital, and TPG, it is perhaps not surprising that this new level of interest has reached China. Additionally, as more Chinese students and professionals come across impact investing abroad (as

[1] A "Active" is defined as having made an investment in the last three years and/or actively looking for investments in China. Firms that have indicated they are exiting operations in China or otherwise discontinuing investment are not included, even if they have invested within the last three years. This number is similar to that reported by the China Social Enterprise and Impact Investment Forum and Narada Foundation's study *China Social Enterprise and Social Investment Landscape Report* (2019).

Table 1 Impact investors currently active in China

Firm name	Domestic/ international	Founded (year)	Headquarters	Website	Investors/ donors	Sector-focus	Geographic focus
98 Sparks (PureTerra)	International	2018	Shanghai	http://98sparks.com/	International	Water	Global
ABC World Asia	International	2019	Singapore	www.abcworld.com.sg	International	Financial and digital inclusion, better health and education, climate and water solutions, sustainable food and agriculture, and smart and livable cities	China, Southeast Asia, South Asia
Dao Ventures	International	2012	Beijing	https://www.daoventures.com/	International and domestic	Food, environment, technology	United States, China
Ehong Capital	Domestic	2007[a]	Shanghai	http://www.ehongcapital.com	Domestic	Sustainable agriculture, energy and environment protection, health and eldercare, quality education	China
Impact Hub Shanghai	Domestic	2017	Shanghai	impacthubshanghai.net	Domestic	Multi-sector	China
Mana Impact Partners	International	2017	Hong Kong	https://www.manaimpact.com/	International	Ocean sustainability, sustainable agriculture, circulate economy	Asia
NPI	Domestic	2006[b]	Shanghai	http://www.npi.org.cn/	Domestic	Multi-sector	China

(continued)

Table 1 (continued)

Firm name	Domestic/ international	Founded (year)	Headquarters	Website	Investors/ donors	Sector-focus	Geographic focus
SA Capital	International	2008	Hong Kong	http://www.sa-capital.com/	International	Education, human resources	Greater China, Southeast Asia
TPG Rise	International	2017	San Francisco	https://therisefund.com/	International	Agriculture and food, education, energy, financial services, healthcare, infrastructure, technology	Global
Tsing Capital	Domestic	2000	Beijing	www.tsingcapital.com/	International and domestic	Clean-tech	China
UOB Venture Management	International	1992[c]	Singapore	https://www.uobgroup.com/	International	Multi-sector	Southeast Asia, China

[a] The Impact fund launched in 2018
[b] Impact fund NPI Social Venture Fund launched in 2016
[c] Impact fund Asia Impact Investment Fund I was launched in 2015

well as in China), they inject new life and energy into initiatives back in China. However, this self-perpetuating cycle of interest only continues if progress in the industry is made. Burnout among existing advocates in the space appears to be common.

Veterans in the space are less convinced by the renewed attention. In our interview, a senior executive of the Sustainable and Impact Investments in Asia of the LGT, noted that interest could not transition into action without additional support. "We have been active in impact investing in Asia, including China, for over a decade. There is huge potential, but there need to be more investor-friendly policies, an enabling ecosystem, and greater incentives to attract increased capital allocation from foreign investors." Additionally, this is not the first instance of increased interest by LPs in China. Jenna Nicholas, CEO of United States-based impact investing consultant Impact Experience, remembered a similar surge of interest from HNWI and family offices in 2016. "There is a lot of interest in impact investing in China, but this interest is not always aligned with the actual investments that are made and the action that is taken."

Perhaps lack of progress is fed by the lack of institutional memory. A senior-level staff of Partnerships and Corporate Innovation at food tech accelerator Bits × Bites recalled the cyclical nature of the social enterprises' space in China. In 2009, he worked at the for-profit social enterprise D. Light China, which provides affordable solar power solutions globally. "At that time, there were so many social entrepreneurs in Beijing getting attention and funding, but they're all gone now. Now I see industry reports rehash these subjects over and over again, forgetting that we had a lot of social enterprises ten years ago."

2.2 *Current Measurement Practices of Impact Investing in China*

Measurement practices in China are fairly underdeveloped. International impact investors such as TPG Rise and ABC World Asia use the international measures normally. Local impact investors are more likely to use qualitative stories or their own impact measures. In an interview, a senior-level staff of Ehong Capital admitted, "Measurement is something that we haven't done so well so far. We only ask the company for very general calculations, such as the percentage of old people they serve and how many of them are living in poverty. Measurement is something we can do better in the future, and we've looked into the measurement tools such as IMP (Impact Measurement Project), IRIS (Impact Reporting and Investment Standards), SROI (Social Return on Investment), and we use 'IRIS+' as a practical tool. But what we believe is that the measurement and calculation is not the critical thing, the key thing is to make the investment so that the business can expand quickly and they can provide impact." Currently, Ehong uses its own measurement framework, but is also using "IRIS+" as a tool.

Many interviewees commented on a need for a tailored or simplified system for China. One anonymous interviewee from a local non-profit focusing on impact measurement noted, "If you want to use measurements in China, you need to change to adjust to the on-the-ground situation. For example, many systems use a founder assessment measure, but expectations of founders are very different in China than in other parts of the world." A senior-level executive of Mana Impact Investment noted in our interview, "I learned 25 different models of impact measurement in the U.K., but we (Mana Impact) want to use a very efficient and simple model. If it's too complicated, it can't be widely implemented." Two active impact investors in our research scope have built a proprietary system, while three have indicated that they measure their impact on a case-by-case or use qualitative measures. Several of the large non-profits, including YouChange, Leping Foundation, and Narada Foundation, are currently focusing on advancing impact measurement (see Table 2).

3 China's Impact Investing Ecosystem

In China's impact investing ecosystem, the roles of government, philanthropy, for-profit companies, and supporting organizations are different from their global counterparts and thus key factors of the ecosystem are also unique. In this section, we analyze the important influences of market factors, policy, financial structures and expectations, culture, support institutions and networks, and human capital.

3.1 Markets

Supply and demand can be viewed from the perspective of the impact investor and the investee company. While we have focused our analysis on the demand and supply in regard to impact investors, we have also provided a brief overview of the supply and demand factors of the investee company in order to better understand the drivers within the overall ecosystem.

3.1.1 Impact Investee Perspective: Demand and Supply of Impact Investing Capital

Because impact investees can be both social enterprises and traditional companies operating in impactful sectors, demand is based on the number of social and environmental issues that these companies are trying to address. China's looming social and economic challenges have been well documented. Interviewees mentioned a range of issues that impact investees address, including China's rapidly aging population, slowing economic growth, food security and sustainable agriculture challenges, and climate change. Additionally, China's national economic development

Table 2 Impact investors on the continuum of capital

	Financial-only	Responsible	j5ustainable		Impact		Impact-only
	Delivering competitive financial returns						
		Mitigating Environmental, Social and Governance (E5G) risks					
			Pusuing Environmental, Social and Governance opportunities				
				Focusing on measurable high-impact solutions			
Focus	Limited or no regard for environmental, social or governance (E5G) practices	Mitigate risky ESG practices in order to protect value	Address proggressive ESG practies that may enhance value	Address societal challenges that generate competitive financial returns for investors	Address societal challenges where returns are as yet unproven	Address societal challenges that require a below-market financial return for investors	Address societal challenges that cannot generate a financial return for investors
Examples		• PE firm integrating ESG risks into im vestment analysis • Ethically-screened investment fund	• "Be st-in class" SRI fund • Long-only public equity fund using deep integration of ESG to create additional value	• Publicly-listed fund dedicated to renewable energy projects (e.g.a wind farm) • Microfinance structured debt fund (e.g. loans to microfinance banks)	• Social Impact Bonds/ development Impact Borids	• Fund providing quasi equity or unsecured debt to social enterprises or chanities	

plans and strategies have laid out a number of ambitious social objectives. Goals related to urbanization, healthcare, green energy, and environmental priorities alone will require USD 8.1 trillion in funds (Koleski 2017). The Chinese government is encouraging private sector participation, and the investees of impact investors can help meet this demand.

In contrast to other popular markets for impact investing, China's government already provides solutions for many issues. For instance, the government already provides most of China's basic infrastructure, and the public already expects many or most social services solutions to come from the government rather than the private sector. Furthermore, public sector solutions are often more effective at creating social impact than social enterprises. As a senior Manager of the Asian Venture Philanthropy Network (AVPN) noted in our interview, "For instance, there was one social enterprise that provided nutritional meals at a national level, but the government found that it was easier to make and deliver meals locally (such as preparing boiled eggs) rather than send these packs to rural areas."

On the supply side of the capital, potential investees have a range of potential funding and are not limited to impact investors. Investees may prefer personal funds, venture philanthropy, loans, grant capital, or even investment from traditional venture capital (VC) or private equity (PE) firms. In fact, some investees may actually avoid funding from an impact investor, as it comes with extra reporting requirements. Additionally, accepting impact investment may have negative consequences for investees because the impact investing label implies a lower return and, whether true or not, may discourage other traditional investors in later funding rounds.[2]

Of course, for many social enterprises, impact investors would be welcomed. Impact investors may be more willing to support companies that traditional VCs would not. An interviewee at sustainable technology investment firm Tsing Capital, remarked, "We made decisions to invest in companies when other investors had not seen their potential. In many cases, we invested in companies during their series A, and we would find that other investors in the market, including other VC firms or corporate ventures, started to pay attention to the technologies and companies, and they decided to invest in the following rounds."

3.1.2 From the Perspective of Impact Investors: Supply and Demand

The need to address the growing number of social and environmental issues is uncontested, and for-profit solutions have a enormous potential to meet this need. For the

[2] A The availability of alternative sources of capital that may be more preferential or impactful than impact investing is an important debate within the impact investing community, but outside of the scope of this report. Per Brest and Born (2013), a particular investment only has impact only if it "increases the quantity or quality of the enterprise's social outcomes beyond what would otherwise have occurred." Their report also outlines a framework for understanding the additionality of an impact investment. In a contrasting view, Miller (2017) argues that the impact delivered by the investee is the most important measurement, regardless of where the capital did or could have come from.

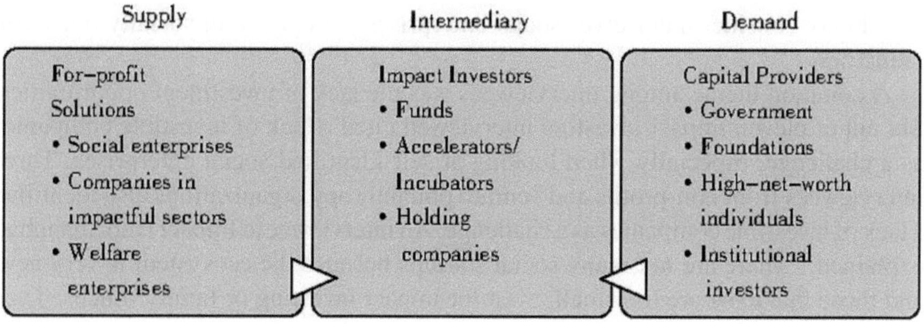

Fig. 1 Impact investors supply and demand

impact investee, demand comes from their consumers and supply of capital from a number of sources. However, for impact investors the supply and demand relationship is switched. Impact investors are meeting the demands of investors and supplying access to invest in these for-profit solutions. In the following, we detail the pressures and influences both on the impact investor supply of suitable investee companies and the demand of investors for impact investing (see Fig. 1).

Impact Investor Supply of Suitable Investee Companies

Globally, impact investors typically (though not always) invest in self-identified social enterprises, given that social entrepreneurs have a social mission and are aligned with impact investors strategically from the beginning. Thus, it is essential to understand the size of the social enterprise market in China to determine whether China has a sufficient supply of investee companies. Per China Social Enterprise and Impact Investment Forum and Narada Foundation's study China Social Enterprise and Social Investment Landscape Report (2019), there is not a single agreed-upon definition of social enterprise in China, and estimates of social enterprises in China drastically change depending on definition. In the lowest range, 234 social enterprises had been certified by the local non-profit China Charity Alliance's China Charity Fair from 2015 to 2019. The number of social enterprises jumped to 1684 when using "self-identification" as the criteria. Finally, when including farmers' co-operatives, private non-enterprise units, and social welfare enterprises, this number increases to 1.75 million. This final definition expands to entities that are generally smaller and community-based, rather than profit-based, and thus typically not suitable for impact investing.

Due to the requirement for financial returns alongside social returns, many social enterprises may not be scalable or profitable enough for impact investors. If impact investors restricted themselves to self-identified social enterprises, their opportunities would be severely limited. Indeed, that is likely why many impact investors (such as Tsing Capital and Ehong) focus primarily on investing in start-ups and companies that do not consider themselves social enterprises but operate in socially impactful industries.

A common theme among interviewees was the lack of investment opportunities. Six out of eleven impact investors interviewed cited a lack of investible companies as a challenge, especially when looking at self-identified social enterprises. Three interviewees from non-profits and venture philanthropy organizations also identified a lack of investible companies as a challenge. An interviewee at Impact Hub Shanghai, explained, "There are not many social startups because the ecosystem is very new, and those that exist are too small, even for impact investing or family offices. They can't find enough start-ups. People are waiting for the start-ups to grow up."

Finance-first impact investors may have a large supply of investment opportunities as they often invest in companies that do not self-identify as social enterprises. Indeed, the most significant impact investment in China is a "traditional" company. TPG Rise, along with two other TPG funds, The Carlyle Group and others, invested USD 1.9 billion into Du Xiaoman Financial.[3] As an interviewee of Ehong Capital explained, "There are a lot of entrepreneurs doing impactful and innovative things, but they don't think of themselves as social entrepreneurs."

The "low hanging fruit" that more financially focused enterprises provide for impact investors may be one of the reasons why there has been an influx of more finance-first investment. Even impact-first investors are looking at more commercially focused enterprises. For example, LGT, along with VC firms Lightspeed China, Steamboat Ventures, and GSR, invested in Mamada V, a leading Chinese e-commerce platform empowering individual mothers to open their online stores to sell educational products. As an interviewee of LGT elaborated, "Although Mamada V did not describe themselves as a 'social enterprise,' we participated in this investment round because the CEO and management team were value-aligned in their mission to improve livelihoods for mothers in China. With the rise of emerging consumers, increased internet, and mobile accessibility, we believe that tech-enabled models like Mamada V are well positioned to deliver robust financial returns coupled with scalable social impact."

NPI is also considering a similar change in strategy due to financial sustainability. An interviewee of NPI noted, "If we want to continue to run this social investment fund, we have to shift from typical social enterprises to companies with good CSR standards that can make a social impact. We need to make sure that this company can grow very big and make profits or can get big enough to attract other investors. Otherwise, you just can't keep it running."

An additional theme that kept arising during interviews was a current lack of successful case studies. Indeed, when assessing whether there is sufficient market supply for impact investing, past case studies provide an important indicator. An interviewee at venture philanthropy organization Venture Avenue, remarked, "If we

---

[3] A There has been some controversy if Du Xiaoman's investment can be considered impact investing, due to the number of traditional investors involved in the deal and its origins as the financial services unit of Baidu. Bank (2018) argues that TPG will be on the hook to deliver impact outperformance at the company level, and thus considers it an impact investment.

want to make impact investing, we need to look at successful case studies, but for the whole industry we've only seen the same few studies for the last five years." While some interviewees listed smaller projects that achieved local success, very few impact investments have reached a national scale. The most commonly cited is China Foundation for Poverty Alleviation (CFPA) Microfinance Management.

Finally, similar to many underdeveloped markets, many interviewees cited a gap between the capital provided and the available opportunities. This is not a new concern. An interviewee of Impact Experience, remembered the first wave of enthusiasm for impact investing. "The size of deals was a really important one. For many investors, the minimum investment size was too big compared to the opportunities. The ability to find deals is a challenge."

This is partially an issue when impact investors are defining which companies to consider. Most institutional capital is looking for larger ticket sizes, and social enterprises are usually too small. Only one self-identified social enterprise, China Foundation for Poverty Alleviation (CFPA) Microfinance Management. More than half of all impact funds (active and inactive) surveyed had an average investment size of USD 5 million and under. Other social enterprises that have reached a national scale (such as Blued) have relied strictly on traditional venture capital investors. Further exploration of CFPA will be outlined in the final part of the study.

Impact Investing Demand of Investors

Demand-side suppliers of capital include governments, foundations, institutional investors, high-net-worth individuals, and retail investors. Many impact investors were identified in China (both active and inactive) with disclosed LPs, seven received funding mostly from HNWI or family offices. One impact investor received capital mainly from foundations. The remainder (mostly international impact investors) were mainly funded by institutional investors such as development finance institutions, multinational corporations, sovereign wealth funds, and pension plans. Local capital providers have mainly consisted of HNWI and foundations, which have traditionally been the early drivers of impact investing in other markets.

HNWIs can consider factors beyond strict financial returns. Reflecting the global trend of millennial perspectives on wealth, impact investing in China is becoming an area of interest as children of China's first wave of successful entrepreneurs—commonly referred to in China as fuerdai (rich second generation)—claim control of their inheritance. Indeed, several interviewees noted that many fuerdai are interested in impact investing. However, not all HNWIs see the benefit of impact investing, instead preferring to set up their own charity or foundation.

Local foundations have been a fundamental source of capital for many venture philanthropists and impact investors around the world. However, most of the capital originates from a small handful of progressive foundations in China. Foundations as a broader source of capital have been challenging to access due to the limited number of grant-giving foundations and perceived risk in foundations investing from their endowment. Only 1% of foundations are grant-making, in comparison to operational foundations that directly engage with constituents (Chu and Wang 2019).

DFIs, which are critical investors in funds in other impact investing markets, are relatively few in China. While DFIs such as the International Finance Corporation and Asian Development Bank are active in China, they have typically invested directly or through traditional private equity funds focused on impactful areas such as clean technology and agriculture but do not consider themselves impact investing funds.

Beside foundations, relatively few impact funds received capital from other types of local institutional investors. Institutional investors, including pension plans, corporations, fund of funds, and asset managers, have invested in impact funds. Several interviewers noted that conversations with institutional investors were met with intense skepticism, especially regarding financial returns. As an interviewee of Calvert Impact Capital, noted, "When you get to institutional investors in China, and you start talking about below market returns, then they just blink."

Government is the largest source of potential capital. Indeed, the government has played a pivotal role as both fund manager and LP in China's domestic private equity industry (Leeds and Satyamurthy 2015) and thus could imaginably be an important source of capital for impact investing as well. Indeed, you see this in the case of green finance, which has had large government support. The Shanghai municipal government once set up a venture philanthropy fund in 2011 (Zhao 2012).

3.2 Policy

Perhaps more than any other market, the government plays an important role in China. The government directives are obviously socially driven and can potentially provide support for impact investors. In addition, some municipal governments have created supporting local policies.

3.2.1 Regulation and Supporting Policies for Social Enterprise and Impact Investing

Currently, there is no national regulation for social enterprises or impact investing. However, new regulation has been passed in many "socially impactful" industries. Two areas often mentioned in particular are green finance and social welfare enterprises.

Government support of alternative energy is well-documented. For instance, the National High-Tech Research and Development program (863 Program), though not directly targeting the creation of an impact investing market, was used to enable innovation in renewable energy and clean tech, natural targets of impact investors (Thornley et al. 2011). The Chinese government's support of green finance also indicates its willingness to support a nascent industry in order to further social or economic goals. In 2016, the Green Finance Task Force, a group of experts from the government, private, non-profit, and academic sectors, released a comprehensive plan to support green finance, including building a green banking system, promoting green funds and bonds, and creating a green rating system, among other initiatives (Green Finance Task Force 2015). China has one of the world's largest carbon exchanges, and in 2020, China had the second-largest issuance of bonds, after the United States (Climate Bonds Initiative 2021). Notable to the development of the green finance sector is that its development was built mostly using a top-down approach. Top-level buy-in would also likely be required for more substantial support for impact investment.

Social welfare enterprises (SWE) are an additional area where there is already existing government support. Social welfare enterprises receive tax benefits depending on the number of disabled workers employed by the enterprise. Unfortunately, 90% of SWE disappeared after China's Open Door Policy in the 1990s, and unfavorable changes in the tax policy in 2007 further diluted their benefit. However, due to the laxer criteria that SWE now need to meet, there is also potential to transform these into more sustainable social enterprises. One Chinese scholar (Zhang 2016) argues that introducing competitive institutional logic (i.e., a market-based, rather than subsidy-reliant approach) into SWE could reverse the decline of SWE and create strong social enterprise (SE) market players. Improving SWE policies can be seen as a more localized and perhaps easier approach to SE policy.

Beyond the green finance sector and SWE, the government has recently passed laws supporting the industries impact investors often invest in, such as education and healthcare (including eldercare). Recent laws include an amendment to the Law of Promoting Privately Run Schools to allow for-profit schools (Hogan Lovells 2016). At the State Council's Executive Meeting in May 2019, Premier Li Keqiang laid out policy incentives such as tax and fee cuts for services in elder care and child care (Zhang 2019). These laws will incentivize investment and can create opportunities for impact investors.

3.2.2 Local Policies

On a local level, several municipal governments have recently set up policy incentive schemes or industrial parks for impact investing or social enterprises in recent years. Four municipal governments, Beijing, Chengdu, Shunde District-Foshan, and Futian District-Shenzhen, have published policies on social enterprise. One Chinese scholar (Pan 2020) argues that Chengdu has done a good job in integrating within all levels of local government. Chengdu municipal government began supporting social enterprises as early as 2017. In 2018, Chengdu created a social enterprise certification program, with 12 companies certified in 2018 and 27 in 2019, and has published nearly 20 specific policies that directly support social enterprises, such as incubation, talent and event support, certification awards, and rent subsidies (Pan 2020).

The Futian District in Shenzhen was one of the municipal governments to specifically support social impact investing in the early stage. In 2017, it released "Instructions of Futian District on Building a Social Impact Investing System" and further guidance on supporting social enterprises in 2018 (AVPN 2019b). While these policies lay out broad areas where Futian can support impact investing, such as the creation of a government guidance fund or giving assistance to supporting organizations, there has not yet been further news on the actual implementation of these policies.

Responses from practitioners have been mixed. An interviewee of NPI believes that local government programs have a huge potential impact. "If you can have several local pilots, it will be easier to push for national policy. Until you have successful local pilots, national regulators won't support impact investing. They heavily rely on the successful pilots to start pushing for supporting policies. Local governments will inspire more cities to adopt this approach." Most of these programs are only a few years old, while those have existed for longer.

3.3 Finance

The financial market is an important indicator of an enabling environment for impact investing. Per Acevedo and Wu (2018), a well-developed financial market is more likely to support impact investing. Additionally, the debt condition can indicate the need for non-governmental sources of capital to address a country's social needs. China's financial market has become increasingly open.

Market-oriented pricing on China's stock and bond markets is also important for the sustainable development of China's financial system. China also launched several smaller exchanges focusing on SMEs, including Second-tier Market, Third-tier Market, and the Growth Enterprise Market.

China's bond market, which has also developed dramatically, mainly issues SOE or government bonds. However, private corporate players are growing, and unlisted companies and SMEs have been allowed to issue bonds since 2012 (Allen et al. 2017).

3.4 Culture

Cultural influences include both civil society's perspectives on how to address social challenges but also their perspectives on the role of investment. As noted by an interviewee of Bits x Bites, "The place of charity is different here than in the West, and so the place of impact investing will be slightly different." Indeed, the understanding of philanthropy and social impact is different in China, given its political, economic, and cultural history.

There are several factors that explain why philanthropy in China's history is relatively small. Firstly, in western society, both the government and charity are major providers of social services. In China, the government is considered, throughout history, one of the main providers of social services. As an interviewee of Asia-focused impact investment firm SA Capital explained, "There are certain sectors in China where people are much more reliant on government or consider this project as very much part of national, provincial, or local plan."

Secondly, the formal non-profit sector is a relatively recent phenomenon. For comparison, in the United States, modern philanthropy began in the early twentieth century. China's formalized philanthropic sector only began with the open-up policy in the late 1970s. It has simply had less time to develop. Because of China's more nascent sector, the public was not as aware of philanthropic activities and its professional opportunities.

In the private sector, the development of China's private equity and venture capital industry creates opportunities for investors. One direct result of China's economic success in the past 20 years is the expectations of traditional investors. Investors in private equity and venture capital in China expect a higher return, a shorter investment period, and a more active role as an LP (EMPEA 2008; Lin 2013).

These ideas around philanthropy and investment undoubtedly affect potential investors' perceptions of impact investing and their likelihood to invest. At first glance, current expectations of both traditional philanthropy and investment at first glance do not align with the ideas of impact investing: many philanthropists want to only consider the social impact, while investors expect quick and high returns. An interviewee of YouChange explained, "For many high-net-worth individuals, impact investing is seen as not generating value because it doesn't have the benefits that donating does. There's no 'good feeling', no recognition, no tax support." An interviewee of Dao Ventures also noted similar impressions from potential investors, "They don't see impact investing as effective means to that end, they see investment as investment and charity as charity." It indicates that these sectors have only existed for decades; subsequent cultural perceptions of social impact and investment are also in their early stage. These ideas are not set in stone, nor do they indicate that impact investing is completely incompatible for investors or philanthropists.

3.5 Supports

Supports are categorized by intermediaries and platforms, and networks. Intermediaries include incubators, accelerators, other capacity builders, and consulting support firms. Platforms and networks include research institutions for impact investing, community development institutions, social exchanges and forums, and crowdfunding and fundraising platforms and funds.

In the past few years, several Chinese local organizations have either added venture philanthropy and impact investing to their main mandate or been established specifically to support the venture philanthropy and impact investing ecosystem. Of these, YouChange, Narada Foundation, and the China Global Philanthropy Institute are perhaps the most vocal. Below is a list of supporting networks and platforms in China (see Table 3).

Table 3 The main supporting organizations for impact investing in China

Organization	Website	Activity
Asian Venture Philanthropy Network (AVPN)	https://avpn.asia/	A regional industry association for venture philanthropy, AVPN in recent years has widened its mandate to include all forms of "social investment", including impact investing. It conducts industry research, holds an annual forum and other events, and is a networking platform
China Alliance of Social Value Investment (CASVI)	https://www.casvi.org/en/	CASVI promotes sustainable finance "through developing social value quantitative assessment system; establishing a platform that connects sustainable investors with investees as well as raising public awareness of the total value in terms of economy, society, and environment"
China Social Enterprise and Impact Investing Forum (CSEIF)	http://www.cseif.cn/index.php	CSEIF holds annual forums and events on social enterprise and impact investing, publishes industry research, and runs the China Social Enterprise and Impact Investment Awards
Corporate Social Responsibility Development Center (CSRDC)	N/A	CSRDC conducts research and holds training on impact investing
Ford Foundation	https://www.fordfoundation.org/	Ford Foundation has supported research reports on impact investing in China
Global Impact Investing Network (GIIN)	https://www.casvi.org/en/	GIIN has conducted several small events in China and Hong Kong
Global Philanthropy Institute (GPI)	http://en.cgpi.org.cn/	GPI holds training programs. Its social finance and innovation center publishes research on impact investing and green finance
Impact Hub Shanghai	https://impacthub.net/	Impact Hub Shanghai, in addition to its own impact investment fund, also hosts education and training events
Narada Foundation	http://www.naradafoundation.org/	Narada is supporting impact investing through reports, venture philanthropy projects, and is currently an LP in an Ehong Capital
RS Group	http://www.rsgroup.asia/about/	RS Group sponsors events and conferences on impact investing

(continued)

Table 3 (continued)

Organization	Website	Activity
Social Enterprise Research Center (SERC)	N/A	SERC conducts research on social enterprises and supports outstanding social enterprises
TBLI Group	https://www.tbligroup.com/	TBLI Group Hosted events or family offices interested in ESG and impact investing
YouChange China Social Entrepreneur Foundation (YouChange Foundation)	http://www.youcheng.org/	YouChange makes grants and mostly provides nonfinancial support to projects

Perhaps notable is that aside from AVPN, most of the support organizations are local. International organizations have historically been less active in China. For many international organizations, the high cost of reaching out and collaborating with China may not be justified by the amount of current activity. An obstacle for international collaboration is the language barrier. As an interviewee of AVPN noted, "Unlike the business sector, the language barrier is still a problem for NGOs and others in the social sector, and makes the international exchange and peer learning a huge challenge for us." Conferences and events in China are highly dependent on translation services and few international reports are translated into Chinese.

On the other hand, Chinese organizations have not joined the international conversation deeply. Very few Chinese organizations are GIIN members, such as Ehong Capital, CSEIF, and Narada Foundation. There are currently no Chinese signatories for IFC's Operating Principals for Impact Management.

Finally, the majority of supporting activity is educational, including industry research and educational events. However, talks and conferences around impact investing are still very basic. At the recent breakout session on "Impact Investing in Asia" at the China Social Enterprise and Impact Investing Forum, few audience members knew the difference between a general partner (GP) and a limited partner (LP). This may be due to the fact that the conferences are oriented more toward (and thus attract more), non-profit practitioners rather than for-profit practitioners.

3.6 Human Capital

The lack of professionals with the necessary skills for impact investing was a challenge that was frequently identified in interviews, both in the context of the impact investors themselves and the investable social enterprises. Per an interviewee of Dao

Ventures, "In social investment space, many come from an NGO background, they don't have an industry background. They really want to do well, but they need a sector focus and can't just have a good heart." An interviewee of the Narada Foundation also commented on the need for the right kind of talent, both on the finance or non-profit side. "Right now, there is no talent available. A lot of investors just want to invest, and those in the impact space don't understand the finance. We need interdisciplinary talent."

Among the eight local impact investors in China surveyed, five have at least one founder with finance experience. Only one of the venture philanthropy organizations surveyed, Mana Impact Investment was founded by someone with a background in finance. This appears to be relatively few compared to global impact investors, whose founders and investment team typically have a finance background. While not a direct comparison, globally four in five impact investors came from pure financial services or for-profit background, with 95% of impact investor roles having some financial services experience (Ferreira et al. 2019). Per the 2019 GIIN Annual Impact Investor survey, 80% of respondents indicated that their investment management staff primarily came from conventional investing and 45% of respondents reported talent was sourced from corporate backgrounds.[4] Additionally, while sufficient human capital remains an issue for impact investors globally, 89% of respondents indicated there had been either significant or some progress regarding "professionals with relevant skill sets."

For impact investors specifically investing in self-proclaimed social enterprises, especially early-stage social enterprises, human capital is an issue at the portfolio level. An interviewee of the Leping Foundation, explained the lack of talent has affected how they source deals. "It is hard to find social enterprises from the NGO sector. Instead, we try to motivate social mission-driven entrepreneurs from the business side." Even impact investors who are more commercially motivated are frustrated with the lack of talent. An interviewee of Tsing Capital remarked, "Oftentimes, When I see financing pitches or roadshows of companies from the philanthropy or social enterprise world, I feel that they lack the business sense and relevant corporate operations experiences to make their idea work, which is actually frustrating for me."

Some investors have seen an improvement over the years. An interviewee of Venture Avenue shared a similar sentiment, but noticed an evolution in the type of talent in the social enterprise space, "It's usually difficult for NGOs to switch their mindset, of 'I don't want to do commercial because it is not pure'. They often don't have enough business skills. Before, most social enterprises arose from non-profit. Now a lot of social enterprises are started by commercial professionals."

[4] A Respondents may source talent from multiple sectors.

4 Conclusion and Recommendations

4.1 Summary

In China, it's easy to get swept away by the potential scale of the opportunity. Talk is easy; action is much more difficult. If impact investing is to reach any meaningful scale in China, advocates must first take a step back and recognize the current state of the impact investment system.

The ecosystem is small, with a few firms making impact investments. A few interviewees could point to successful case studies, with China Foundation for Poverty Alleviation (CFPA) Microfinance Management being the most often cited.

Impact investors face a number of challenges, including LP misperceptions, lack of clarity around definition and standardization, a lack of support infrastructure, and a dearth of qualified investment professionals.

Impact measurement systems are underdeveloped. Most impact investors either did not have a measurement system in place, or they used their own simplified framework (usually qualitative), making it difficult to objectively evaluate impact. Several interviewees cited a need for simplified or tailored standards for China.

There is a dearth of professional investment talent in the ecosystem. Impact investing, as well as venture philanthropy, professionals in China with traditional investment backgrounds are fewer in number than those in other impact investing markets.

At the same time, the dominant narrative of impact investing is more associated with venture philanthropy and traditional philanthropy than an investment with potential for returns. This is likely due to the influence of early international advocators like the British Council and the fact the most vocal local advocates of impact investing are foundations and venture philanthropists, such as YouChange, the China Global Philanthropy Institute, and the Narada Foundation.

However, recent activity from global commercially focused impact investors, including TPG Rise and Temasek's ABC World Asia Fund, as well as Narada's support of Ehong Capital, indicate a shift toward more commercially oriented investing. Early impact-first investors have realized that they need financial sustainability, something that investing in more community-oriented and impact-focused social enterprises often cannot achieve. Furthermore, traditional investors have seen the success of global impact investment funds and are eager to join the bandwagon.

Many impact investors have focused on early-stage investments, and the current most popular sector strategies are sustainable food/ agriculture and the environment (including clean-tech, water solutions, and sustainable consumption). The most often cited opportunities for investment by interviewees (which include venture philanthropists) included healthcare (specifically elder care), environment, rural development, and agriculture.

4.2 *Suggestions*

There are several suggestions for building the industry that have been identified. First, clarity is still needed around the definition of impact investing (especially in the context of venture philanthropy, ESG, and responsible investing). There is a lot of confusion around the definition of impact investing, even among those most actively engaged in the sector. Research and dissemination of the most current perspectives around the definition of impact investing, such as IFC's Operating Principles for Impact Management, can also help impact investors stay in touch with progress in the global community.

Second, in tandem with coalescing around a common definition, international impact investors and international impact institutions, especially the large brand name investors such as TPG Rise and ABC Asia, should engage with the local impact investing community. A concerted effort must be made to share best practices and involve China in the discussion on impact investment in the international community.

Third, venture philanthropy and grant funding should focus on building up the ecosystem's support system and developing social enterprises with scalable potential. Venture philanthropy can be used to de-risk commercially sustainable social enterprises with large-scale potential and build up a pipeline for future impact investments. Grant funding is essential for building out the ecosystem's infrastructure, including measurement systems, research, accelerators, incubators, and education programs.

Fourth, while training non-profit talent is important, impact investors also need to focus on attracting more talent from the private sector. The philanthropy sector in China is in many ways as nascent as impact investing and is only just starting to professionalize as an industry. This makes it even more challenging to source appropriate talent from the philanthropy sector for impact investing. Instead, efforts should be concentrated on attracting private-sector talent. Collaborating with universities, especially business schools, to introduce young talent to impact investing can help build out the talent bench for the future. At the same time, partnering with businesses to "rent" talent through externships or sabbaticals could be ways to fill in current talent gaps. This could also double as a means to expose more professionals to impact investing.

Finally, government support is necessary for impact investing to scale, which requires coordinated and active advocacy as an industry. The evolution of the green finance industry in China is a successful case study and could be used as a guide. Additionally, given the large overlap in themes and ethos with green finance, increased communication, and partnership with key players in green finance could benefit both industries.

References

ABC World Asia (2019) ABC World Asia closes new $385 million fund. ABC World Asia. https://www.abcworld.com.sg/media-releases/abc-world-asia-closes-new-s385-million-fund/

Allen F, Qian J, Gu X (2017) An overview of China's financial system. Annu Rev Financ Econ 9(1):191–231. https://doi.org/10.1146/annurev-financial-112116-025652

AVPN (2019b) Social investment landscape in Asia: China. https://avpn.asia/si-landscape/country/china/

Bank D (2018) The era of impact-washing is over. Medium, 5 May. https://medium.com/@davidmbank/the-era-of-impact-washing-is-over-55071a6a7793

Bouton L (2018) Toniic, partner of GIIN, wants to bring impact investing to China's wealthy Rivera. Financial Times, 3 December. https://www.ft.com/content/23f02dd0-f3c9-11e8-9623-d7f9881e729f

Brest P, Born K (2013) Unpacking the impact in impact investing. Stanf Soc Innov Rev. https://ssir.org/articles/entry/unpacking_the_impact_in_impact_investing

British Council (2016) Key actors in China's social enterprise sector. https://www.britishcouncil.cn/en/uk-china-social-enterprise-social-investment-partners

China Social Enterprise and Impact Investment Forum and Narada Foundation (2019) China social Enterprise and Social Investment Landscape Report 2019. China Social Enterprise and Impact Investment Forum and Narada Foundation

Chu P, Wang O (2019) Philanthropy in China. Asian Venture Capital Association. https://avpn.asia/insights/philanthropy-in-china/

Emerging Markets Private Equity Association (2008) EMPEA EM PE quarterly review. Emerging Markets Private Equity Association IV(2):Q2

Emerging Markets Private Equity Association (2019) 1H 2019 data. Emerging Markets Private Equity Association

Ferreira L, Harrison KB, Wiersum J et al (2019) Impact goes mainstream: talent trends in the age of impact investing. Russell Reynolds Associates. https://www.russellreynolds.com/insights/thought-leadership/impact-goes-mainstream-talent-trends-in-the-age-of-impact-investing

FinNews Asia (2019) UOB launches second impact fund. FinNews Asia, 11 June. https://www.finews.asia/finance/28943-uob-launches-second-impact-fund

Green Finance Task Force (2015) Establishing China's green financial system. The People's Bank of China, UNEP, Green Finance Task Force

International Center for Not-for-Profit Law (2019) Non-profit law in China. Council on Foundations. https://www.cof.org/content/nonprofit-law-china

Koleski K (2017) The 13th five-year plan. U.S.-China Economic and Security Review Commission. https://www.uscc.gov/sites/default/files/Research/The%2013th%20Five-Year%20Plan_Final_2.14.17_Updated%20(002).pdf

Leeds R, Satyamurthy N (2015) Private equity investing in emerging markets: opportunities for value creation. Palgrave MacMillan, London

Li D (2019) Interviewed by Rae Winborn. NPI Social Venture Interview

Lin L (2013) The private equity limited partnership in China: a critical evaluation of active limited partners. J Corp Law Stud 13:185–217

Lovells H (2016) China to allow for-profit schools, except in compulsory education. Hogan Lovells Publications. 13 December. https://www.hoganlovells.com/en/publications/china-to-allow-for-profit-schools-except-in-compulsory-education

Lv R (2019) Interviewed by Rae Winborn. Impact Hub Shanghai Interview

Miller C (2017) Big league: transforming the capital markets with impact rigor and disclosure. Impact Alpha. 28 September. https://impactalpha.com/big-league-transforming-the-capital-markets-with-impact-rigor-and-disclosure-750b6537d6f2/

Pan S (2020) The development of social enterprise in China Chengdu City's innovative practice. Acad Entrepr J 26(2)

TPG Rise (2018) The rise fund leads series C financing in CFPA microfinance. TPG Rise. https://therisefund.com/news/rise-fund-leads-series-c-financing-cfpa-microfinance-chinas-leading-rural-microfinance
Rivera Acevedo J, Wu M (2018) A proposed framework to analyze the impact investing ecosystem in a cross-country perspective. Rev Eur Stud 10(4):87–113
Roque R (2020) Interviewed by Rae Winborn. SA Capital Interview
RS Group (2016) RS group impact report. RS Group. http://report.rsgroup.asia/#download
Thornley B, Wood D, Grace K, Sullivant S (2011) Impact investing: a framework for policy design and analysis. Pacific Community Ventures, Initiative for Responsible Investment at Harvard University, The Rockefeller Foundation. http://www.pacificcommunityventures.org/wp-content/uploads/sites/6/2015/07/Impact_Investing_Policy_Full_Report.pdf
Xu A (2019) Interviewed by Rae Winborn. Asian Venture Philanthropy Network Interview
YouChange China Social Entrepreneur Foundation and China Development Research Foundation (2016) China Social Impact Investment Report 2016. YouChange China Social Entrepreneur Foundation, China Development Research Foundation
Zhang X (2016) Institutional transition from welfare enterprise to social enterprise: the localization of legislation and policy in Chinese context. J Inst Stud 8(1):121–131
Zhang Y (2019) Multi-pronged support for community-based elderly care, childcare, domestic services. The State Council The People's Republic of China. http://english.www.gov.cn/premier/news/2019/05/29/content_281476688627618.htm
Zhao M (2012) The social enterprise emerges in China. Stanf Soc Innov Rev 10(2)
Zheng A (2019) Interviewed by Rae Winborn. China Impact Ventures Interview

Case Study of Impact Investing in China: CD Finance

Since 2005, CD Finance has become the leading microcredit company continuously driven by the mission to address poverty alleviation and village vitalization issues through a commercial approach. By the end of 2020, CD Finance had accumulatively disbursed over RMB 74 billion Yuan loans to millions of low and mid-income customers in rural China who otherwise did not have access to formal loans. To better serve rural households and businesses, its services have expanded beyond microcredit to a package of comprehensive services, including agricultural input supply, agricultural product procurement, and agricultural technical assistance. CD Finance has helped millions of rural people at the bottom of the pyramid increase income, weather shocks, pursue opportunities, and live a better life. In China's microfinance industry, where many players are driven purely by commercial profits and deviate from serving microentrepreneurs, CD Finance is a rare example that keeps mission firmly in mind and pursues long-term value instead of short-term profit. The concern for rural customers is a part of the company's DNA.

Besides impacts on its customers, CD Finance also has made significant impacts on the industry of financial inclusion in China. Its success demonstrates the business case of adopting the market-based and commercial approaches to address the financial inclusion issues. It has proved that microfinance institution is able to achieve both of financial returns and social impacts. The company's quick growth, profitability, and impacts have attracted interest from many types of investors, including impact investors and traditional investors. Amid the world's pandemic crises, CD Finance still secured investment deals from five new investors. Because of its success, CD Finance has won numerous awards. In 2016, it was certified by the China Charity Fair as the first Gold Medal Social Enterprise in China. In 2017, CD Finance was awarded Annual Social Enterprise by the China Social Enterprise and Social Investment Forum. It was the first winner of the award. In March 2021, it was named Fortune China's top 20 most socially impactful companies.

There is no shortage of case studies in the global impact investing industry, but the case studies in China are scarce. This is the purpose of this case study, telling stories about what lies behind a successful social venture like CD Finance, transforming from

Finance Center for South-South Cooperation, *Impact Investing*,
https://doi.org/10.1007/978-981-99-4935-9_4

a dying NGO program to a leading mission-driven business that is fully attractive for both traditional investors and impact investors. The case study will analyze how CD Finance's investors leverage the power of their capital differently, why they chose CD Finance for impact investment, what value initiatives they created for CD Finance beyond the capital, and how they helped CD Finance scale better fulfill the mission and achieve a stronger return. Both investors' and investees' perspectives are woven together in this impact investing success story, which illustrates how impact investing can help solve societal problems in an effective way.

The case study will also draw lessons from the growth of impact investing in global microfinance, which is an important context and enabler for impact investing in CD Finance. Microfinance is one of the most developed sectors for impact investing. The key lesson learned from the impact investing in microfinance is that strengthening the meaningfulness of impact investing calls for collaborated efforts not only from impact investors and social ventures, but also a supporting ecosystem to include industry associations, collaboration networks, standard setters, rating companies, performance benchmarking database, regulators, etc. The case study of CD Finance offers a wealth of lessons and experiences for the industry of impact investing in China.

1 Impact Investing, Microfinance, and Financial Inclusion

Microfinance investment is an impact investing strategy that targets specifically the microfinance sector. It emerged and surged even before the term impact investing was created (CGAP 2013). Initially, impact investing concentrated in the field of microfinance, as only microfinance had a proven track record of profitability and social impacts. In 2013, microfinance made up close to three-fourths of total impact investing in developing countries (GIIN 2014). A McKinsey report found that among the 48 impact investor exits between 2010 and 2015 in India, 31 were in financial inclusion and "nearly 80% of the exits in financial inclusion were in the top two-thirds of performance" (Pandit and Tamhane 2018). From 2015, with global micro-finance institutions maturing and growth rate decreasing, impact investors started to allocate capital across a broader range of sectors, such as energy, water, sanitation, food, agriculture, and healthcare, reflecting the overall diversity of impact investing strategy.

Microfinance seeks to provide financial services for the segment of the working poor that are excluded from formal financial services. This population is often called the unserved and underserved, many of whom are smallholder farmers, self-employed, or operating a small business. Providing financial services helps low-income families build assets, increase income, manage risks, pursue opportunities, and smooth consumption. Microfinance investment aims to achieve the double bottom line as the industry calls—financial return and social performance, which are equivalently important.

The growth and commercial evolution of microfinance spanned three decades. The success of the microfinance industry has busted the myth that impacts investing's financial return has to be sacrificed for social impacts. "Never before has so much capital been directly targeted at the bottom of the pyramid, relying significantly on market mechanisms rather than governments" (Warwick et al. 2015). Understanding the evolution of global microfinance will provide the important context to understand the growth of CD Finance and the roles of its investors played. It will also help draw lessons for the development of impact investing in other sectors.

Microfinance institutions (MFI) started to be community-based not-for-profit or non-governmental organizations (NGOs) in the 1970s. Initially, the emphasis of MFIs and the microfinance sector was mostly on poverty alleviation and social impacts. They were funded by subsidies, grants, and soft loans on noncommercial terms from donors and philanthropic investors. The grant and subsidy helped MFIs increase capacity and developed solid business models to be financially viable and achieve independence of subsidy, laying the basis for commercialization.

Starting in the mid-1990s, the commercialization of the microfinance industry truly took off with successful MFIs achieving institutional profitability. With investment from philanthropy organizations and international development financial institutions (DFI), leading MFIs were transformed from NGOs to financial institutions regulated by national banking supervisors, making possible large-scale financial outreach to the low-income populations, while operating profitably. DFIs, also known as development banks or development finance companies, "is a multilateral, bilateral or government-backed institution that invests in the private sector for development purposes" (GIIN 2021). They provide capital for a business that generate both financial and social returns. Examples of DFIs are IFC (the financing arm of the World Bank), FMO (a Dutch development bank managing funds for the Dutch Government), IDB (Inter-American Development Bank), and KfW (a German state-owned development bank).

A few prominent microfinance institutions quickly gain international traction such as BancoSol in Bolivia, Acleda in Cambodia, Compartamos in Mexico, and Equity Bank in Kenya. Each of these institutions was transformed from small NGOs into a large-scale commercial institution, quickly scaling up to reach and serve a very large number of the working poor. These institutions at the forefront proved that microfinance institutions were able to achieve both financial returns and social impacts. The success stories inspired a number of social entrepreneurs across different countries (including the founding team of CD Finance) to build commercialized microfinance business models and also attracted investors with social responsibility.

By 2005, the commercialization of microfinance had been well developed globally, and capital investment in microfinance surged. The investors expanded beyond a small group of philanthropy and development finance institutions. Successful IPOs of the top-performing microfinance institutions, such as Compartamos, attracted mainstream commercial investors. Private investment funds specifically for microfinance, known as Microfinance Investment Vehicle (MIV), were established, including individual investors and institutional investors with social responsibility. MIVs further drove the surge in private capital investment in microfinance. Mainstream investors such as pension funds started to invest in microfinance.

Before MFIs became investment-ready institutions, philanthropy organizations and DFIs played a pioneering and catalyst role in helping microfinance succeed by providing seed capital to early-stage and high-risk microfinance institutions, providing grant and technical assistance to build institutions' capacity and business models, and establishing an ecosystem that supported the growth and commercialization of microfinance. As Lieberman (2020) pointed out, "more than the success of microfinance on purely commercial terms, the role of subsidies—not for market-distorting price reductions, but rather for innovation, benchmarking, and infrastructure and capacity building—is perhaps the most salient feature of microfinance in fostering emerging business models that aim for social impact. Over time, however, the subsidy element in microfinance has diminished considerably, and most commercialized MFIs operate at present without substantial subsidies."

In the growth journey of CD Finance, philanthropy organizations and DFIs also played a critical role in transforming the institution from a small NGO program to a profitable business. As the company matures and builds a track record, with the continued involvement of DFIs, it starts to pull in funding from impact investors and later becomes attractive to mainstream investors such as pension funds.

2 The Emergence and Evolution of CD Finance

The global success in microcredit brings the model to China. From the 1990s, the United Nations Development Program (UNDP) and the World Bank began promoting the concept of microcredit in cooperation with the Chinese government and organizations in China. Small pilot programs were established based on the Grameen Bank model, which had gained international visibility. In 1996, a World Bank's microcredit program was launched in Qin-ba Mountainous Area of China, together with the Foreign Capital Project Management Center under the State Council's Poverty Alleviation Office. This was the origin of CD Finance.

But when the commercialization of microfinance was well developed in other countries, microfinance in China was still program-based, lack of sustainability and viability, and heavily relying on government subsidies and donor grants. Inspired by the global success of the commercialized microfinance model in poverty alleviation, the Chinese government started to change its regulatory environment, encouraging the commercialization of microcredit services in order to increase credit access for the working poor.

In 2005, the People's Bank of China (PBOC) initiated a pilot program in five western provinces to establish microcredit companies (MCC). In 2008, China Banking Regulatory Commission (CBRC) and PBOC jointly issued a notice, allowing MCCs to establish nationwide, which officially started the commercialization of microcredit in a large-scale. In the meantime, global MIVs started actively looking for investment opportunities in China, with the expectation to build a demonstration model that can replicate the success of Compartamos in Mexico, BancoSol in Bolivia, and Acleda Bank in Cambodia. The favorable regulatory policy and growing interest from the international microfinance community in China's market provide critical enabling factors for the growth of CD Finance.

CD Finance is the epitome of microcredit development in China. In 2000, after the microcredit pilot program in Qin-ba mountainous area ended, the World Bank and the Foreign Capital Project Management Center decided to hand over the program to China Foundation for Poverty Alleviation (CFPA), an NGO which is supported by the government. CFPA then established a microcredit department to manage the program. The microcredit department spun off in 2008. It became an independently operated microcredit company named CD Finance, which has been one of the earliest microcredit companies adopting the commercial approach in China.

Box 1: China Foundation for Poverty Alleviation (CFPA)

CFPA, established in 1989, is a non-governmental organization in China, supervised by the State Council Leading Group Office of Poverty Alleviation and Development. Its programs are focused on poverty alleviation, health, education, disaster relief, rural development, and international development. Over the past 32 years, CFPA has been widely recognized as one of the top NGOs in China with strong social influence. At the end of 2019, CFPA has raised a total of 6.7 billion RMB in poverty alleviation funds, benefiting over 40 million people from the poverty-stricken and disaster-hit areas.

Source CFPA website, https://www.cfpa.org.cn/.

Today, CD Finance is recognized as one of the largest and most influential mission-driven enterprises in China that specializes in serving the rural population. Understanding CD Finance's growth path will help highlight what contributes to its success and what may be needed for other aspiring social enterprises to grow into a business that can attract investment from impact investors and even traditional investors.

The development of CD Finance encompasses three key stages:

- Achieving self-sufficiency and commercialization (2000–2008)
- Demonstrating profitability and impact at a scale (2009–2016)
- Transforming into a comprehensive service platform (since 2017).

In different stages, different types of investors help CD Finance achieve stronger financial performance and social impacts as the company evolves. In stage one, concessionary impact investors play a critical role in seeding and de-risking CD Finance, helping establish a viable business model and achieve self-sufficiency. In stage two, non-concessionary impact investors joined the efforts to help CD Finance quickly scale operations, refine processes, and develop skills in balancing financial returns with social impact. In stage three, with the joining of mainstream investors,

CD Finance is able to launch systematic transformation and further expand the breadth and depth of services.

2.1 Achieving Self-sufficiency and Commercialization (2000–2008)

Save the Dying NGO Programs

Between 2000 and 2004, CFPA Foundation's microcredit program was struggling. At that time, only four out of ten microcredit projects were still in operation. Even those four projects heavily relied on government subsidies and grants to survive.

The business model was collaborating with the local government's poverty alleviation offices for program operations. Since CFPA foundation did not directly monitor and control branch operations (from staff hiring to the use of funds), loan quality quickly deteriorated, fraud increased, and the program heavily relied upon government subsidies and external donations.

In January 2005, Mr. Liu Dongwen was appointed as the director of the CFPA's Microcredit Department. As the first step toward reform, CFPA Foundation transformed the business models and built the foundation's own branches, directly reporting to the headquarter in Beijing, strengthening the internal control of operations in the field. The reform stirred up conflicts with local governments, but the foundation successfully managed the transformation. Once internal control was strengthened, the loan performance improved quickly.

Achieve the Commercialization

As the first step toward commercialization, CD Finance started to raise funds from the commercial market instead of seeking donations in order to place internal pressure to increase operational efficiency. Thanks to the connection of CFPA, three new funding sources were secured. In 2005, the Hong Kong-based Kadoorie Charitable Foundation offered two options for assistance to CFPA's microcredit program: 2 million RMB as a donation or 10 million RMB as an interest-free loan. The microcredit department chose the latter. In 2006, CFPA was able to obtain a loan of 100 million RMB from CDB at the commercial interest rate.

In 2007, after seeing the news on the collaboration between CFPA and CDB, Standard Chartered China contacted the CFPA to provide a commercial loan of 20 million RMB, and then another 20 million RMB in 2008. Standard Chartered had provided debt funding to microfinance institutions in other countries and was excited to identify similar opportunities in China.

The new sources of funding, especially access to the commercial capital, significantly contributed to the CFPA microcredit program's independence of grant and improved the financial sustainability (see Table 1). By 2007, CFPA microfinance

Table 1 Loan received in early stage of CD Finance

Year	Institutions name	Institution type	Amount (000 RMB)	Funding type
2006	Kadoorie Charitable Foundation	NGO	10,000	Loan interest-free
2006	China Development Bank	DFI	100,000	Commercial loan
2007	Standard Charter Bank	Commercial bank	20,000	Commercial loan
2008	Standard Charter Bank	Commercial bank	20,000	Commercial loan
2008	Danone Group	For-profit business	20,000	Loan interest-free

programs had successfully achieved financial self-sufficiency.[1] In November 2008, the CFPA microfinance department was spun off to be an independently operated company. CD Finance was hence officially launched as a limited liability company with CFPA being the only shareholder. By the end of 2008, CD Finance had 195 employees, 26,878 clients, and 26 branches. The largest goal then was to reach a total disbursement of 1 billion RMB, which was achieved only five years later.

2.2 *Demonstrating Profitability and Impact at Scale (2009–2016)*

- **Quick scaling up**

After being spun off as an independent company and structured as a for-profit company, CD Finance moved to the next chapter, which was to demonstrate profitability and impact at scale. This was the period that CD Finance achieved fast scaling-up at an average growth rate of 52% for consecutive eight years. By the end of 2016, active clients had increased by ten times compared to 2009, and the loan portfolio had jumped by 25 times (see Table 2).

- **Strengthen operation and governance**

To enable quick expansion, CD Finance further strengthened internal governance, streamlined the operations, and improved the standardization. CD Finance hired local loan officers who might not have high education but had strong local knowledge and connections with excellent communication skills to build the relationship and win the trust of a farmer. Products and processes were highly standardized so that loan officers with low education could easily understand and follow.

[1] In Microfinance, financial self-sufficiency is defined as revenue that is able to cover expenses, not including revenue from any kinds of grant, donation, and subsidy.

Table 2 Growth of CD Finance (2009–2016)

Year	2009	2010	2011	2012	2013	2014	2015	2016
Number of employees	298	494	650	830	1251	1860	2377	3101
Number of active borrowers	36,428	67,241	106,491	130,683	174,557	237,817	306,101	366,401
Loan portfolio (in thousands of yuan)	107,043	187,970	389,138	660,811	856,191	1,181,457	1,872,155	2,609,667
Loan portfolio growth rate (%)	76	107	70	30	38	58	39	67

Source Collected from CD Finance by our research team

Business departments such as internal control, marketing, credit management, risk management, and training center were established one after another in the headquarter, providing professional guidance and quality control for local branches in the credit process. CD Finance also developed a loan tracking system in-house to improve operation efficiency.

- **Increase profitability and impacts**

From 2009 to 2016, CD Finance's profitability quickly increased with the growing customer base and excellent loan quality. ROE increased from 0.28% in 2008 to 9.25% in 2016, and ROA increased from 0.13 to 1.68%. It was also the period that the microfinance industry in China entered a booming period. But many players in the industry deviated from targeting underserved customers. They operated similarly to traditional financial service providers and did not target "micro" segments with small loans.

Different from those players, CD Finance remained truly committed to serving the vulnerable groups in the rural area. Table 3 demonstrates the increased outreach to the low-income, rural, women, and low-education clients. During 2009–2016, the average loan size as a percentage of GNI per capital had been stable between 25 and 30%. The loan size as a percentage of GNI per capita is a commonly used indicator in microfinance to measure how deep MFIs reach down in national income distribution. The indicator demonstrates that CD Finance's clients are consistently in the low-income level. Other indicators show that the percentage of clients in poor counties had been more than 80%, and rural, women and low-education client percentage had been above 90%. CD Finance's success in this stage challenged the conventional view that social enterprises cannot be scaled to create attractive returns.

Table 3 Profitability and outreach depth of CD Finance (2009–2016)

Year	2009	2010	2011	2012	2013	2014	2015	2016
Number of active borrower	36,428	67,241	106,491	130,683	174,557	237,817	306,101	366,401
Average loan amount (RMB)	6679	8612	9657	9859	10,279	11,333	12,743	16,760
Average loan size as % of GNI per capita (%)	27	30	30	26	25	24	25	30
Rural client percentage (%)	99	99	99	99	98	97	95	94
Women client percentage (%)	–	–	91	93	93	94	93	92
Percentage of clients in state-designated poor counties (%)	–	–	92	92	80	81	85	81
Clients with education at middle school or below (%)	–	–	95	95	95	94	93	92
ROA (%)	0.13	2.78	3.35	1.62	1.32	1.04	1.29	1.68
ROE (%)	0.28	6.58	9.32	5.64	4.16	3.48	5.47	9.25
Portfolio at risk (>30 days) (%)	–	0.05	0.61	0.23	0.8	0.27	0.83	0.77

Source Collected from CD Finance by our research team

During this stage, CD Finance also increasingly expanded the product offerings from group loans to individual working capital loans, agricultural loans, and non-financial services such as emergency relief, agricultural technical support, and financial education, in order to increase client financial capability and help them generate more income. A social performance management working group was set up and social performance elements started to be incorporated into everyday business processes from 2011 in order to ensure social impacts along with the financial return.

2.3 *Transforming into a Comprehensive Service Platform (Since 2017)*

(1) **Pivot business model by digital transformation**

Adapting to the changing market dynamics, CD Finance started to rethink, redefine, and revamp its business model. The company decided to transform into a comprehensive service platform for rural farmers enabled by digital channels. One of the motivations behind the transformation is that CD Finance recognizes that microcredit on its own is not enough to well serve the poor who need comprehensive forms of intervention. Beyond microcredit, rural farmers also have a huge demand for the opportunity to improve agricultural production skills, access reliable channels to acquire quality agricultural inputs, and gain marketing support to sell agricultural products. With the outreach to over 400,000 clients, CD Finance decided to do more for its clients. Offering a diverse array of financial and non-financial services will not only better help rural farmers increase their lives, but also help CD Finance diversify its own income and deepen impacts (see Table 4).

Another motivation for transformation is the trend of leveraging digital technology and social media, which prompted CD Finance to transform the way they do business and interact with customers. In 2017, after intense internal debate, the company decided to launch a mobile application called *Zhong He Jin Fu*, aiming to increase the access and convenience of using loan products for the rural population. Six months later, the App went live. In 2020, CD Finance launched an integrated digital service platform called *Xiang Zhu*, and as of August 2021, the number of *Xiang Zhu* application downloads is over 4 million. The platform encompasses almost every aspect of rural life, ranging from agricultural input purchase, agricultural production assistance, agricultural product e-commerce to financing, insurance, emergency relief, and local community merchant information. Figure 1 is a snapshot of the *Xiangzhu* application showing diverse functions of the platform.

Table 4 Diversified services provided by CD Finance

Services	Year of service started	Description
Microcredit	2000	Provide microcredit for farmers and rural small businesses
Agricultural technical assistance	2009	Provide technical knowledge and advice to farmers in agricultural production
Microinsurance	2009	Provide free accident insurance for farmers
Emergency relief	2010	Provide emergency relief funds for farmers
E-commerce of agricultural products	2019	Connect farmers directly with end consumers
Procurement of agricultural products	2019	Procure agricultural products from farmers and sell to large supermarkets, catering enterprises, and traders
E-commerce of agricultural inputs	2020	Sell quality agricultural inputs to farmers at a competitive price
Local community service	2021	Provide local service (such as cell phone top-up and local business information) to the rural population

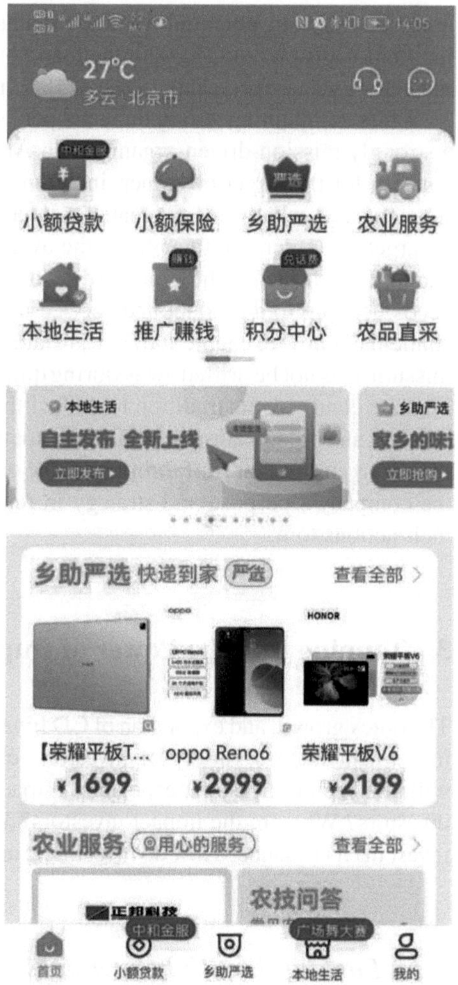

Fig. 1 Snapshot of the *Xiangzhu* App

While launching the digital transformation, CD Finance does not fixate on the "digital" component. They understand young and digital native clients would prefer smooth "no-touch" or "limited-touch" customer experience, but middle-aged and low-education clients would prefer a "high touch" customer support due to the lack of digital skills and confidence. The company adopts a combination of human touch and digital technology with loan officers offering human touch to increase the underserved segment's knowledge and skills in using digital financial products so that clients can truly benefit from digital finance.

(2) **Maintain strong profitability while being client-centric**

In this stage, CD Finance has continued to maintain its stellar business and financial performance. Its profitability track record, innovative business models, as well as long-term growth potential attracted mainstream investors both within China and internationally. As of Q4 2020, the loan portfolio reached 12.2 billion RMB, which indicates a year-over-year increase of 10% in a special year plagued by the pandemic.

While maintaining strong financial performance, CD Finance has continued to be a strongly mission-driven organization. At the heart of the company's mission is a concern for the target customer, including a clear understanding of who the target segments are, what value to create for target customers, and how to deliver the value to target customers. In this phase, the average loan size as a percentage of GNI per capita is around 35%. The strategic direction consistently has been driven by customer needs, leading to a product and service mix that is unique in the marketplace. The challenge is how to enable staff to translate the mission into practice and to ensure the mission does not be drifted away during quick expansion and growth. In this stage, CD Finance continues its tradition to embed the values into staff training, management process, and organizational culture. Company-wide discussions were initiated several rounds to ensure that staff throughout the organization have a clear understanding of the company's purpose and strategy in relation to customer centricity and to align their actions to it.

3 Tapping into the Power of Impact Investors

The quick growth and expansion of CD Finance would not have been realized without investment from a variety of investors, especially impact investors. This section will analyze on investors, especially impact investors, of CD Finance: Who are the investors? Who are the impact investors? Why did these impact investors decide to invest in CD Finance? How do investment approaches differ among impact investors?

3.1 Looking for Right Investors

The section is going to examine the equity and debt investors of CD Finance and explain the pre-investment strategies that CD Finance and investors adopt for alignment.

(1) **Current and past investors**

CD Finance's unique market positioning and excellent track record of profitability and impacts have attracted a wide variety of domestic and overseas investors. The three Tables 5, 6 and 7 demonstrate the variety of equity and debt investors for CD Finance, ranging from international Development Financial Institutions (DFIs), venture capital, foreign and domestic commercial banks, Microfinance Investment Vehicles (MIVs), institutional investors, etc. Over 70% of past and current equity and debt investors are impact investors, which demonstrates the significant role that impact investors have played in the growth of CD Finance.

Table 5 Equity investors of CD Finance as of August 2021

Institution name	Impact investor	Investment time (year)
China Foundation for Poverty Alleviation (CFPA)	Y	2008
International Financial Corporation (IFC)	Y	2010 and 2016
Sequoia China	N	2010
Ant Financial	N	2016
High Impact Capital Advisors (HICA)	Y	2017 and 2020
The Rise Fund under TPG	Y	2018
Ningbo Renda Puhui Investment Management Partners	Y	2018
NewQuest Asia Fund	N	2020
Stream contribution	Y	2020
ABC World Asia	Y	2020
Teachers' Innovation Platform under Ontario Teachers' Pension Plan	N	2021

Note IFC and CFPA successfully exited in 2020

Table 6 Main international debt investors of CD Finance as of August 2021

Institution name	Impact investors	Investor type	Earliest investment time (year)	Current or not
Beijing Bank	N	Commercial bank	2011	Y
China Merchant Bank	N	Commercial bank	2013	Until 2015
China Zheshang Bank	N	Commercial bank	2015	Until 2016
Bank of China	N	Commercial bank	2020	Y
Gansu Financial Holding	N	Financial group	2020	Y
Beijing Zhongguancun Bank	N	Commercial bank	2020	Y
Xiamen International Bank	N	Commercial bank	2020	Y
China Guangfa Bank	N	Commercial bank	2021	Y

Table 7 Main domestic debt investors of CD Finance as of August 2021

Institution name	Impact investors	Investor type	Earliest investment time (year)	Current or not
IFC	Y	Development finance institution	2014	Y
BNP Paribas	N	Commercial bank	2015	Ended in 2020
Asia Development Bank	Y	Development finance institution	2016	Y
ResponsAbility	Y	Microfinance investment vehicle	2017	Y
Symbiotics	Y	Microfinance investment vehicle	2018	Y
Incofin	Y	Microfinance investment vehicle	2019	Y
DEG	Y	Development finance institution	2019	Y
GLS Alternative Investments	Y	Microfinance investment vehicle	2020	Y
Proparco	Y	Development finance institution	2020	Y

The two Tables 6 and 7 demonstrate an interesting comparison of debt investor profiles of CD Finance: international debt investors are mainly Development Financial Institutions (DFIs) and Specialized Microfinance Investment Vehicles (MIVs), the typical type of impact investors in microfinance; and domestic debt investors are all financial investors such as commercial banks and financial groups.

(2) **Pre-investment strategies for alignment**

As shown above, CD Finance has different profiles of investors ranging from venture capital, DFIs, institutional investors, foundations, and as a result, the expectations of financial returns and impacts vary. Some investors accept below-market-rate financial returns and would like to maximize social impacts. Some investors expect financial returns at the market rates while pursuing social impacts. Despite the differences in expectations, there is high alignment among CD Finance's investors on the company's strategic direction and value propositions. According to CD Finance, there was no tension or conflict at the board level. Although some investors do hope the company can increase profitability, they still place more emphasis on the long-term value instead of short-term profits. The company is never forced to dilute its focus on the social mission for the benefits of higher profits. There is consensus among shareholders that the company's niche market positioning is to serve the rural low and middle-income populations. The high alignment is attributed to the pre-investment strategy that CD Finance conducted to ensure the investors' alignment on organizational mission, vision, and goals.

CD Finance has created three *must-to-have* criteria for the investor profile:

- **Mission alignment**: the potential investors need to have strong buy-in for CD Finance's vision, mission, and value propositions. Social mission plays an important role in moderating the relationship between investors and CD Finance and the relationship among different investors.
- **Value to add**: the potential investors need to bring the resources and add the value as needed by CD Finance. CD Finance seeks an investment of time, knowledge, skills, network, and other resources from their investors, which are equally important as investment capital. The past and current investors of CD Finance have created different values to help bring CD Finance to the next level, which will be explained in the next section.
- **Market-based approach**: the potential investors can adhere to market-based approach and will not be subject to political interference. The key lesson that CD Finance learned from its NGO-program stage is that government intervention could disrupt the effective distribution of resources and internal management.

CD Finance used to reject several big-name institutional investors because of being unfit for the criteria. Not only does CD Finance strive to ensure the mission alignment, but also the impact investors. The due diligence undertaken by impact investors is different from that among traditional investors. The primary focus of commercial due diligence is on profitability, scalability, market competitiveness, and a profitable exit opportunity. But during the due diligence process of impact investors, investors reflect if the investee's mission, vision, actions, and culture are aligned with investors, so that in the post-investment the possibility of non-alignment, tensions, or conflicts will be at a minimum level.

Steven Ying, the founding partner of High Impact Capital, explained how different investors achieve alignment in the interview: "We minimize the conflict and tensions between financial returns and impact from the beginning by ensuring there is a strong alignment among investors regardless of their intentions. Impact investor wants to achieve impacts which need innovative solutions to the world's social and environmental problems. (Traditional) financial investor sees the value creation in solving world problems. I think we are in agreement whether you are an impact investor or (traditional) financial investor, it's time to put our money in companies to solve the problems that matter to the world."

Impact investors also plan for a responsible exit strategy. For example, when IFC exited in 2020, they identified buyers that were aligned with the company's mission and made sure the buyers recognized the commercial value in serving low-income consumers, as well as the impact inherent in these business models.

Except for three must-to-have criteria, there is also a nice-to-have criteria, which is sector knowledge. CD Finance finds it much easier to attain an alignment with impact investors with deep knowledge or experiences in microfinance. Almost all of CD Finance's international debt and equity investors have deep microfinance knowledge and experience in other countries. Investing in CD Finance is their first investment in China's microfinance. For example, IFC is a pioneering impact investor in microfinance. TPG's co-managing partner has years of industry experience in microfinance. Even Sequoia, a typical venture capital, had a previous successful investment in India's microfinance before investing in CD Finance. Sequoia India's investment in microfinance institutions inspired Sequoia China to look for similar investees. Standard Chartered Bank, as one of the earliest debt investors for CD Finance, already had a long history of lending to microfinance institutions in other countries. The deep industry knowledge contributes to alignment, reduces frictions and risk, and helps the social business in designing a viable strategy that is critical to future success.

In financial inclusion investments, the sector knowledge of investors can have significant implications for both impacts and profitability. For example, if a microfinance institution is acquired by an investor with little experience with underbanked customers, the investor could push to increase loan sizes beyond what clients are able to pay back, ultimately leading them into over-indebtedness and resulting in deteriorating loan quality. Or the investor could push to deviate from lending to the underbanked, leading to the mission drift and resulting in the loss of competitive advantage in the market. The industry has witnessed both situations happening in many countries.

Compared to the success of securing international investors, CD Finance has encountered some challenges in seeking domestic investors due to the lack of sector knowledge among domestic investors. Before 2010, few people in China had even heard of the commercial microfinance model. Lending to the poor was associated with subsided interest rates and philanthropy. It was hard for CD Finance to explain the business model: what the mission-driven enterprise is, why they charge a commercial interest rates to the low-income population, and why it is important for them to be profitable to be able to sustainably serve the low-income, etc.

Ten years later, the commercialized microfinance industry in China entered a booming period, and microfinance evolved into financial inclusion. However, the "wait-and-see" government approach and loosening regulation on market entry and practices allowed both good and ill-intentioned players in the market. Many microcredit companies deviated from targeting underserved customers. Rampant growth of some irresponsible P2P and cash loan companies, who targeted the vulnerable group and called themselves "microfinance" or "financial inclusion company", brought serious issues of fraud, over-lending, and illegal collection. These issues have tarnished the reputation of microfinance and financial inclusion. CD Finance's challenges become how to distinguish themselves from those irresponsible lenders.

Ms. Zhen Li, Vice President of CD Finance, explained the challenges in seeking domestic investors in the interview: "It was so much easier to communicate with foreign investors with deep sector knowledge and experiences, as they already have years of investment experiences in microfinance, understand the microfinance business models, and understand how a strong-performing microfinance company should look like. But when we communicate with domestic investors, we often have to spend a lot of time explaining to our business model because there are no industry data for benchmarking. Because of the existence of some irresponsible lenders and a market mixed with good players and bad players, we also need to spend lots of time distinguishing ourselves from those irresponsible lenders and addressing potential investors' concerns."

3.2 *Snapshots of CD Finance's Impact Investors*

This section provides a snapshot overview of three representative impact investors of CD Finance: International Financial Corporation, High Impact Capital Advisors, and The Rise Fund. They respectively invest in different stages of CD Finance business growth. The section will also examine the similarity and differences in the investment approaches of these three investors.

(1) **International Financial Corporation (IFC)**

IFC is one of the earliest investors after the CFPA Foundation. Globally IFC has played an important role in pioneering commercial microfinance since the 1990s. As a leading development financial institution, it acts as an anchor investor and also provides advisory services to early-stage microfinance institutions, helping them create a commercially viable business model and supporting them to scale up and respond to unmet financing demand. It helps demonstrate the business case for commercial microfinance and promotes it as an asset class to attract private institutional investors.

As one of the first investors in 2007, in addition to the capital support, IFC played a critical role in guiding CD Finance to build a strong business model and to enhance governance and operation through technical assistance programs and advisory services in the early stage. IFC has provided debt financing since 2014, which marked the beginning of the foreign debt financing for CD Finance.

IFC also contributed to making the microfinance industry in China more sustainable and responsible through a series of targeted investment and advisory programs. IFC is already one of the largest microfinance investors in China. In the past decade, IFC has invested around USD 800 million in 8 microfinance projects in China.

Box 2: International Financial Corporation (IFC)

IFC, as a private sector arm of the World Bank Group with the mission to promote development through investment in private sector. It is owned by 184 member countries and has global presence in 100 countries, working with 2000 private sector clients. To achieve the mission, IFC offers solutions through direct and indirect investments and advisory services to support early-stage social ventures in developing countries that "are creating new markets, transforming industries, and driving inclusive growth while realizing strong growth." IFC does not pay dividends or taxes. Profits are channeled back into investments in developing member countries. IFC has been a development partner for China for the past forty years, adapting to the country's changing needs over a period of unprecedented growth. Since its first investment in 1985, IFC has supported over 400 private sector projects across China as of June 30, 2020. Currently China is IFC's second largest portfolio country with an outstanding portfolio of USD 3793 million. These projects have archived impressive development results, benefiting millions of farmers and micro, small and medium-sized enterprises (MSME), and raising environmental standards.

Source IFC China Office, https://www.ifc.org.

IFC exited in 2020, the 10th year after it invested in CD Finance. IFC acclaimed in the written interview conducted by our research team that "during the investment holding period (2010–2020), the investment generated both satisfactory financial returns and strong developmental impact. The number of outstanding borrowers increased from around 100,000 to 427,000, the annual disbursement increased from RMB 596 million to RMB 17 billion, and the outstanding loan portfolios increased from RMB 389 million to RMB 12.2 billion. The trajectory of its business growth and healthy financial performance also helped the company attract additional reputable investors to invest in the company and to promote the development of rural finance in China."

(2) **High Impact Capital Advisors (HICA)**

Established in 2011 and based in Hong Kong, China, HICA is a bouquet impact financial advisor specialized in providing non-bank financial institutions (NBFIs) with social and green capitals. It is passionate about deploying capital to solve social or environmental problems that matter to the world. Three principles are imperative to its impact investing approach: the principle of intentionality, the principle of additionality linking the desired effect with the investment, and the principle of measurability. HICA aims to focus investment in areas where no subsidies are required and remain insufficiently served by traditional capital markets while enabling faster progress toward the United Nations Sustainable Development Goals.

HICA invested in CD Finance respectively in 2017 and 2020. Steven Ying, the Founding Partner of HICA, learned of CD Finance in 2013, when there were more than 9000 microcredit companies (MCC) in China. He recalled in the personal interview: "back then, CD Finance was relatively a smaller MCC compared to what it is now. Many people perceive the MCC industry as unattractive, especially how the industry has been portrayed in the media. We thought even if 99.9% of all MCCs were no good, there would still be 9 good MCCs of 9000. We should do our homework and find out which 9 MCC are good." Steven Ying quickly found CD Finance looked impressive for the following reasons:

- **Potential to scale**: it is the only microcredit company that has a physical presence in more than 17 provinces.
- **Leadership**: the core leadership and management team has been very stable with a solid performance track record.

- **Financial performance**: over ten years of consistent financial growth while keeping non-performing loans at a very low level (the ratio for PAR > 30 days never exceeds 2%).
- **Social mission**: address gender inequality and rural poverty issues by empowering rural women to form their own businesses and improve their livelihoods.
- **Business model hard to replicate**: the deep trust between loan officers and clients is extremely valuable and hard to replicate by other institutions in a short time.

According to HICA, on a mark-to-market basis, the investment in CD Finance has yielded an annualized internal rate of return (IRR) greater than the PE industry average of 18% in the same period as of December 2020.

Besides CD Finance, HICA has also invested in other non-bank financial institutions in China and provided these NBFIs with social or green capitals in the form of private debt and private equity totaling the US $500 million since 2017. HICA believes making an impact and making a profit are not mutually exclusive. Steven Ying said in the interview, "There is a general perception that impacts investing meant having to sacrifice returns in exchange for a 'feel-good' outcome. We reject this myth. We believe profit and impact can go hand in hand. We aim to focus in areas where no subsidies are required and remain insufficiently served by traditional capital markets while enabling faster progress towards SDG."

(3) **The Rise Fund under TPG**

TPG is one of the world's largest private equity investment institutions, managing funds across a range of asset classes, including private equity, growth equity, impact investing, real estate, secondaries, and public equity. With more than $100 billion assets under management and 12 offices worldwide as of August 2021, TPG is one of the largest investment firms globally. In 2016, TPG launched The Rise Fund, the global impact fund committed to achieving social and environmental impacts alongside a financial return. With over $5.5 billion assets under management, The Rise Fund invests in growth stage, high potential, mission-driven enterprises across sectors of education, financial services, healthcare, energy, technology, environment protection, food, and agriculture. "Rise would have a lifespan of ten years, with the possibility of up to two one-year extensions. It would target financial return by typical of TPG's other private equity funds" (Gandhi et al. 2018).

In 2018, The Rise Fund investe d in CD Finance. Chang Sun, Managing Partner of TPG China and one of the pioneers in China's private equity industry, explained the reason to invest in CD Finance during the interview conducted by our research team: "CD Finance has a strong track record of success as one of the few profitable microcredit companies in China operating at scale throughout the country with deep customer relationships. Given that most of CD Finance's customers come from China's poorest communities, the impact of their microloans is quite transformative. With loan products that are designed to suit rural, low-income borrowers, CD Finance's customers have the ability to improve the productivity of their businesses and generate savings for the future or invest in crucial services for their families—like education and healthcare—that lead to long-term economic gains. Chinese farmers who take out agricultural loads with CD Finance can see productivity on their farms rise more than 75%."

In addition to CD Finance, The Rise Fund has a number of other investments across China, including a leading online art education platform in China, a fintech company that uses artificial intelligence to provide short-term lending across China, and a fast-growing plant-based protein platform. The Rise Fund also sets out to improve accountability in impact investing for the industry overall. It has dedicated significant resources to developing an impact underwriting systems and tools.

(4) **Different Investment Approaches**

As shown from the snapshots of CD Finance's investors, the practices and approaches associated with impact investing could vary considerably because the motivations, expectations, and ways to define social impacts and financial return are different (see Table 8).

There are differences in sectors that impact investors are interested in. Investors might choose one or multiple sectors that they have deep expertise in, such as healthcare, education, financial inclusion, climate change, etc. The investment team would take a thematic approach first to sourcing or identifying potential portfolio companies. Investors' expectations for financial return and social return are different. Some pioneering impact investors accept trade-offs of financial return and social return in supporting high-potential mission-driven enterprises. Other investors believe that impact investing does not have to be concessionary and focuses only on "win–win" opportunities that generate competitive financial and social returns.

Investors' risk tolerance and preferences for investee business stages are different. Some investors only invest in the early-stage companies as they believe that is where they can add the most value. They are willing to take a high risk to exchange for bigger impacts. Other investors with a lower level of risk tolerance only invest in the growth-stage companies with proven track records. In terms of measurement of social impacts, impact investors use various available tools, indicator sets, and standards. Some collaborated with external partners to design elaborate measurement systems and evaluate the impacts. Some design and conduct the measurement internally. Table 8 summarizes the similarity and differences of investment approaches among CD Finance's major impact investors.

3.3 Key Factors to Attract Impact Investment

CD Finance has gone through a long journey to where it stands in the rural service ecosystem in China. What is the secret receipt that has made CD Finance fully attractive to both impact and traditional investors? In the interviews conducted by our research team, CD Finance's investors revealed these common factors that attracted them: addressing social problems, profitable business models, visionary social entrepreneur, cohesive and committed team, and customer-centered innovation.

Table 8 Investment approaches of CD Finance impact investors

	IFC	The rise fund	HICA
Investment products	Loans, bonds, equity, mezzanine	Equity investment	Equity and debt investment
Investee business stage	In all stages	Growth stage	Growth stage
Financial return expectation	Benchmark to market rate return	Market rate return	Market rate return
Risk tolerance	Medium to high	Medium	Medium
Strategic sectors to invest	Infrastructure, agriculture, financial inclusion, climate, health, and education	Education, financial services, health, energy, technology, environment protection, food, and agriculture	green finance financial inclusion health
Social impact measurement indicators	Developed in-house	Developed in partnership with partners	Customize the existing measurement tools such as MIX social performance tools, the Smart Campaign tool, etc.
Evaluation of social impacts	Internal evaluation	Through the independent company Y analytics	Internal evaluation verified by a third party
Alignment with UN SDGs (sustainable development goals)	Integral to IFC's mandate are SDG 1 and 10. IFC's investment and advisory in sectors aligned with SDG 2, 3, 4, 6, 7, and 9. Across sectors and regions, IFC seeks to promote SDG 8, 5, 12	Portfolio companies are aligned with every SDG goal	Portfolio companies are aligned with SDG 1, 2, 5, 7, 8, 13

(1) **Addressing Social Problem in Large Scale**

One of the first factors that CD Finance's impact investors look at is if the company is trying to solve a problem, if the problem is large enough, if the nature of the solution is scalable, and if the company fully understands and is passionate about solving the problem. CD Finance started with addressing the financial inclusion problem in rural areas as rural farmers and entrepreneurs face a serious lack of access to capital. With CD Finance becoming the largest microcredit institution targeting the rural low-income populations, its vision expands beyond financial inclusion and to broader rural vitalization issues. For impact investors, CD Finance's business model could improve the livelihood of the rural population, narrow the income gap, increase the resilience of farmers against natural disasters, and increase gender equality for middle-aged rural women. For traditional financial investors, solving a societal problem in a large-scale means a largely unmet market demand and business opportunity.

(2) **Profitability and Scalability Model**

Solving problems is important and equally important is the capacity to make profits, to grow, and scale. Making profits is essential for a social business to grow and scale in the long term. The second factor that CD Finance attracted traditional and impact investors is the established user basis and consistent revenue figure. When most investors invested in CD Finance, the company had proven that they were prepared for success on a larger scale. The ROA and ROE have steadily increased since 2014 with excellent portfolio quality and a large customer base. The only exception is IFC and Sequoia China. When they invested in CD Finance, the company had not established a strong record yet. However, both IFC and Sequoia had known microfinance in other countries so well that they believed that CD Finance has the potential to quickly achieve the scale and higher profits.

(3) **Visionary Social Entrepreneur and Committed Team**

Effective leadership is essential to the success of any business, and for social enterprises, it is especially important. A visionary social entrepreneur is very committed and plays a key role in institutional success. This is an important feature not only for the microfinance industry but also for other social ventures. It is also the case of CD Finance.

Much of CD Finance's success could be attributed to Dongwen Liu, who was the key leader in crafting the commercialization blueprint, constantly on the lookout for new ways to solve rural problems and create value for rural farmers. He has been committed to tackling social issues through a commercial approach since the early days of his career. To achieve the transformation, Mr. Dongwen Liu is willing to navigate uncertainty. Facing the ever-changing market and regulatory environment, he is able to grasp new concepts and explore ways of doing things differently.

For a mission-driven enterprise, building strong products and valuable solutions is essential, but creating an engaged and committed team, who will deliver the solutions in the right way, is also the key to accelerating the success much more quickly and sustaining the success longer. As a result of cohesive culture, the employee team at CD Finance is very stable. The average tenure of mid and senior-level managers at CD Finance is over five years (see Table 9).

Table 9 Average tenure of managers at CD finance as of August 2021

	Company history (years)	Headquarter (years)	Regional offices (years)
Senior-level managers	13	7.54	10
Entry and mid-level managers		6.26	8.73

All of the investors closely watch the background of the team to see if they work well as a unit to develop and implement the company's strategy if they would be able to wade through the tough periods together, and if they have the deep market awareness and experiences. Mr. Dongwen Liu explained the team cohesion in the personal interview on March 16, 2021. "We are not owners of the company, but we always use the same entrepreneurial spirit as if we were the owners of the company. We are a group of people who do not purely pursue profits or high salaries. We work to follow our passion, address social problems, and create value for the society."

(4) **Custom-Centered Innovation**

Adaptability and innovation need to start with the demands of clients. It is about adapting to the changing needs of customers and finding innovative solutions to address problems faced by clients. One of the key success factors for CD Finance is its ability to quickly pivot itself around the customer need.

When the rise of smartphone penetration rate in rural areas enabled the underserved population to use mobile phones to access and use various products and services, CD Finance quickly adopted digital approaches to better serve the rural population. But they did not blindly follow the trend of digital transformation. They realized that digital finance could contribute to, but is not able to fully close, the accessibility gap in China. Many clients at the bottom of the pyramid still need human touch (especially face-to-face) to build trust with the digital finance platform, to establish the legitimacy of the product, and to solve problems in using the product. CD Finance decided that a combination of "offline + online" mode (in other words, a combination of human touch and digital technology) is necessary and critical to reach and serve the vast underserved population in the last mile (see Fig. 2).

Online mode refers to mobile application, *Xiangzhu*, as well as the application of technology such as cloud computing, data analytics, and biometrics in the digital platform, improving the efficiency and convenience of using financial products for farmers. Offline mode refers to the team of 6000 employees in over 300 branches who focus on creating a long-term relationship with customers, communicating with

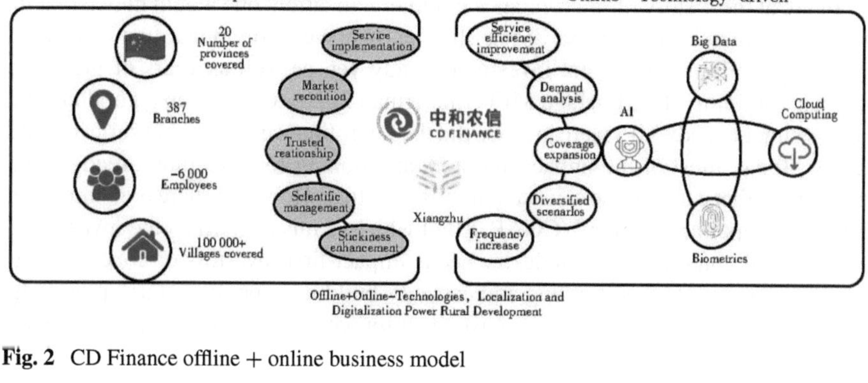

Fig. 2 CD Finance offline + online business model

clients face-to-face, and providing in-person support to clients. The offline mode helps to build up underserved segment's business, finance, and digital skills, ultimately helping them to be more included, and fully benefit from the digital ecosystem. CD Finance understands that being customer-centric while agilely adapting itself to the changing environment will enable the company to be successful in the long term. The vast potential from the unique combination of "offline + online" business models has attracted both impact and mainstream investors.

4 The Role of Impact Investors

For emerging mission-driven business, capital in the monetary sense is the first and foremost need to finance growth. But for the business to grow, social ventures often need other support, including strategic direction guidance, business-building support, and support from enabling ecosystems. So far, CD Finance's investors have offered a range of value-add services to build the business in areas such as product innovation, staff capacity building, talent acquisition, technology advancement, networking opportunities, business development, digital transformation, strategic direction, etc. The value created by impact investors not only filled in internal skills and resource gaps of CD Finance, but also contributed to building an industry ecosystem as a necessary context for the healthy growth of a company. The value created by impact investors can be categorized in the following three areas:

- Build an investment-ready institution in early stage;
- Enhance company value in growth and expansion stage;
- Build an industry ecosystem to enable the investment.

4.1 Building an Investment-Ready Institution in the Early Stage

Looking at the history of microfinance commercialization, one would notice that the investment in microfinance only took off after many years of impact-first investment in young MFIs that were not investment-ready yet, as well as years of grants for capacity building of early-stage MFI (Lieberman 2020). Only when a good number of investment-ready MFI were in place did the microfinance investment surge (CGAP 2013). Today most of the impact investors are looking for investment-ready social enterprises that can provide at least market-rate return. However, there is an important phase of "pipeline creation" (CGAP 2013) which is missing. To create investment-ready social enterprises, the industry needs impact-first investors or concessionary investors to provide seed funding and capacity-building support to start-up or early-stage social enterprises so that they have the resources and guidance to build business models and establish track records which can attract investors looking for market-rate financial returns.

IFC provided years of technical assistance and advisory services for CD Finance to optimize product offering and process and build the internal capacity. The need for capacity building was first identified during the due diligence process. IFC deal team assessed the investee's capacities across governance, operations, and finance. In 2011, right after the investment, IFC committed $1 million as technical assistance funding to hire a group of local and international consultants to provide comprehensive business-building service for CD Finance, including the following scope of work:

- Design agricultural product;
- Optimize individual working capital loan product and process;
- Build risk management department and internal control system;
- Develop credit scoring;
- Launch training center, cultivate internal trainers, and develop internal training materials.

As a result, CD Finance successfully built a risk management system and culture, launched an agricultural loan product, optimized working capital loan, and improved staff technical and management capacity, which led to revenue generation, operational improvements, and risk reduction.

Except for business-building services from its investors, CD Finance also received lots of grants from philanthropy organizations and corporate with social responsibility in the early stage. The major grants and soft loans that CD Finance received were in the early stage. These grants helped CD Finance address funding challenges, increase staff capacity, and provide value-added services to the farmer. See Table 10.

It is interesting to note that only foreign donors were willing to donate grants for institutional capacity building, while domestic donors were more willing to see the funds being used for end clients, either on-lending or other programs that directly benefited the end clients. Except for advisory services and grants, CD Finance also received the third kind of business-building support, which is sponsored study tours and exposure trips to visit the top-performing MFIs in other countries due to the lack of demonstration models in China (see Table 11).

4.2 *Enhancing Company Value for Next-Level Growth*

Besides building the business to be an investment-ready institution, CD Finance's investors also supply human and relational capital for CD Finance to enhance the company value and grow quickly to the next level. Relational capital refers to the relationship with potential investors, business partners, and talents. CD Finance's investors have a rich network of relationships in relevant business sectors and investment communities. When it comes to follow-on rounds of funding, existing investors act as the lead investor and introduce new investors. Investors also help CD Finance

Table 10 Main grant and soft loans CD Finance received in the early stage (2006–2009)

Grant	Institution	Type	Amount (thousand yuan)	Type of funding	Purpose
2007	Give2Asia	NGO	498	Grant	Staff capacity building farmer training on-lending
2007	JP Morgan	Investment bank	250	Grant	On-lending farmer training
2007	Mercy corps	Global NGO	897	Grant	Staff capacity building on-lending
2007	Shell Foundation	Corporate foundation	148	Grant	Women microentrepreneur capability building
Grant	Institution	Type	Amount (thousand yuan)	Type of funding	Purpose
2008	Shell China	Corporate	8970	Grant	On-lending farmer training
2008	Danone Group	Corporate	20,000	Soft loan	On-lending
2009	Danone Group	Corporate	20,000	Soft loan	On-lending

Table 11 Exposure trips/study tours sponsored by donors and investors

Year	Country visited	Institution visited	Funders
2006	Kyrgyzstan	Kompanion	Mercy corps
2008	Cambodia	Acleda Bank	IFC
2010	Mongolia	Xac Bank	Citi
2011	Cambodia	Acleda Bank	Citi
2011	Peru Columbia	Compartamos Mibanco	Citi
2012	Indonesia	Several Indonesian Microfinance Institutions	IFC
2013	Kenya	Equity Bank, Mpesa	IFC

establish new partnering relationships. These relationships are very valuable for CD Finance as otherwise, it would have taken years to establish.

Investors could provide advisory services to CD Finance based on the company's business needs. For example, TPG introduced a talent to CD Finance to lead the newly established microinsurance business. Another investor seconded technology talents to CD Finance to help launch the digital transformation. Because of investors' solid reputation and connections, CD Finance was able to identify and attract talents whom otherwise is very difficult for the company to hire.

Chang Sun of TPG explained the value provided to CD Finance in the interview: "Throughout our investment period, we leverage our expertise in the capital market to help the company deliver highly complicated new financing; Operationally, we bridged resources in multiple areas to solidify its core business and explore new business to support the rural populations, which helps the company to grow into a comprehensive service provider in rural areas."

Investors also organize experience sharing among investee institutions, which is another kind of relational capital. In 2016, IFC introduced CD Finance to become a partner of the World Bank Group's Universal Financial Access 2020 Initiative (UFA 2020), demonstrating its long-term commitment to expand financial services for the "last mile" in rural China.

The key lesson to be learned from CD Finance's experiences is that social venture needs to look beyond mere supply of capital in choosing investors. Rather, a social business should evaluate any investment proposition from a variety of value-add perspectives. By helping CD Finance more widely connected with investors, talents, partners, and other key industry players, investors reduce its own investment risk and amplify the investment return and impacts.

4.3 *Building an Industry Ecosystem*

Another important value created by impact investors is the support to build a healthy industry ecosystem, specifically the microfinance ecosystem in the case of CD Finance, which fueled the growth and investment in commercialized microfinance. GIIN pointed out that one of the four practices defining impact investing is contributing to the growth of the industry, which is specifically defined as "investors with credible impact investing practices use shared industry terms, conventions, and indicators for describing their impact strategies, goals, and performance. They also share learnings where possible to enable others to learn from their experience as to what actually contributes to social and environmental benefit" (GIIN 2019).

One lesson that impact investors can learn from the history of microfinance and financial inclusion is the importance of creating an industry ecosystem and building a strong industry. The ecosystem for microfinance and financial inclusion succeeded in promoting industry transparency, establishing best practices, and fueling investments in the sector (Lieberman 2020).

In the financial inclusion ecosystem, the following players are the major components, sponsored by philanthropy institutions and endorsed by major impact investors:

(1) **Industry data disclosure platforms**: Such as the Microfinance Information Exchange (MIX). MIX was the leading global database for the sector of financial inclusion and microfinance based on self-reported information from thousands of financial service providers is including CD Finance. MIX allowed financial and social performance benchmarking across regions and institutions. It helped unlock billions of impact investing capital to the sector of microfinance. CD Finance was one of the few financial service providers in China reporting to MIX

every year, allowing potential impact investors to benchmark its performance. Several investors such as HICA and IFC used MIX to benchmark financial and social performance.

(2) **Social performance standard setter**: Examples are client protection principles, standards, and indicators set by the Smart Campaign; The Universal Standards for Social Performance Management set by Social Performance Task Force (SPTF). These standards provide best practices to guide financial service providers to implement social performance standards into day-to-day operations and achieve social goals (SPTF 2021). They also provide standard ways for impact investors and financial service providers to measure, report, and compare social performance and client protection in financial inclusion. CD Finance has adhered to the global social performance and client protection standards since 2012, which helped demonstrate its social impacts to potential investors.

(3) **Microfinance rating agencies**: Between 1997 and 2000, four leading specialized microfinance rating agencies were established, which are MicroRate, M-CRIL, Planet Rating, and MicroFinanza Rating (Abrams 2012). CD Finance received the Planet ratings twice, which helped demonstrate its impacts and benchmark financial and social performance for global impact investors. Impact investors also rely on rating agencies to understand the performance of potential investees.

(4) **Specialized Microfinance Investment Vehicles (MIVs)**: These MIVs specifically focus on microfinance investment and enable channeling large volumes of investments into MFI, including CD Finance. Top MIVs include ResponsAbility, Symbiotics, Incofin, and GLS Alternative Investments, which are all debt investors of CD Finance.

(5) **Industry association or collaboration network**: Such as national and international collaboration network. CD Finance has benefited from the global and local network by learning from the best practices, connecting with peer institutions, and increasing exposure in the international microfinance community. Impact investors also actively share learnings within these networks to enable others to learn from their experiences.

Currently, CD Finance's impactor investors are actively contributing to building an impact investing ecosystem. Noticing the key challenges in being lack of impact management standards and discipline in the industry, IFC, in consultation with external stakeholders, developed and launched the Operating Principles for Impact Management in 2019, which established a common discipline "for investors for the design and implementation of their impact management systems, ensuring that impact considerations are integrated throughout the investment lifecycle" (Impact Principles 2021). Based on GIIN impact measurement survey finding in 2020, 26% of investors surveyed have adopted the IFC Operating Principles.

5 Managing and Measuring Impact Results

The core to the impact investing work is the commitment to understanding and improving impact. Managing and measuring impact is critical for both social ventures and impact investors to ensure they are achieving their desired impact results. Impact measurement is also the key to distinguishing impact investing from conventional investing. But unlike the measurement of financial return, there are no universally accepted social impact management and measurement standards.

Today, in the microfinance and financial inclusion industry, there is a universal standard for defining and measuring social impacts, which is called the Universal Standards for Social Performance. But the standards were not established from day one. "Social performance back then, like impact investment today, meant whatever anyone said it meant … Without universal standards, the public understandably concluded that 'social performance' was nothing more than a marketing slogan" (Foose and Folan 2016).

In 2005, the Social Performance Task Force (SPTF) was created, which launched the universal standards for impact measurement and provided a platform to promote best practices for the industry. It took ten years and intensive collaboration among all the major stakeholders for the microfinance industry to widely adopt the Universal Standards for Social Performance (Foose and Folan 2016).

In impact investment, industry players have recognized the shortcomings and have committed the resources to improve impact measurement and management for the industry. As mentioned in the last section, IFC and TPG have made great progress in developing impact management principles and measurement systems. The measurement system enables the investors to assess the level of expected impact before investment, establish impact targets, monitor the progress, and evaluate and report the achievement of impact after the investment.

This section is going to shed light on how CD Finance and its investors measure social impacts. While the sophistication of approaches varies from one to the next, impact measurement is core to both impact investors and social enterprises.

5.1 The Constitution of Impacts

Before introducing different ways to measure impacts, it is best to outline what results, and changes are defined as an impact. Many organizations understand the ultimate changes they wish to bring, for example, improving livelihood and addressing inequalities, which are real impacts. But these changes could take a long time to happen, and there are many small changes that need to happen first, which is called "outcome." Table 12 summarizes the differences among inputs, activities, outputs, outcomes, and impacts, which are key terms to understand the results at different levels.

Table 12 The social results hierarchy—from inputs to impacts

	Definition (Twersky et al. 2010)	Examples	Value	Difficulty to measure
Inputs	The resources used to implement activities	• Funding • Personnel	This is part of the implementation but not the change	Easy to measure
Activities	The processes or actions taken to achieve outputs and move toward outcomes	• Market research • Product design • Communication with clients	This is part of the implementation but not the change	Easy to measure
Outputs	Direct products and services provided to clients	• Loans disbursed • Training provided • Quality seeds and fertilizers provided	The first level of results but not necessarily produce changes	Easy to measure
Outcome	Immediate observable and measurable changes on the beneficiaries	• Improve knowledge and skills • Increase business sales and profits • Increase agricultural production outputs	The second level of results and meaningful changes for the target beneficiaries	Moderate difficult to measure
Impact	Ultimate sustainable changes for a population or a community	• Increase household livelihood • Achieve financial health • Empower women social status	The end results that social enterprises hope to accomplish	Very difficult to measure

In a broad definition, impacts may refer to any results of social enterprises' products and services. However, in a narrow definition, impact only refers to the ultimate changes, which is the long-term effect of an outcome, may involve subjective feeling, and hence is much more difficult to measure. Outputs and outcomes can be used as a proxy for impact where a relationship has been demonstrated through research (Twersky et al. 2010). According to the GIIN survey, most of the impact investors measure the outputs (91%) and outcomes (78%) (GIIN 2019).

5.2 *How CD Finance Manages and Measures Impacts*

CD Finance has adhered to the Universal Standards for Social Performance Management since 2012. The Universal Standards enjoy credibility and wide adoption. They include six dimensions: "define and monitor social goals; ensure board, management, and employee commitment to social goals; design products, services, and delivery channels that meet clients' needs and preferences; treat client responsibly; treat employees responsibly; balance social and financial performance" (SPTF 2021). The Client Protection Standards set by the Smart Campaign are represented in the Universal Standards.

CD Finance is the first microfinance institution in China to create a specialized social performance committee and working group to strategize and monitor social performance work. The working group submits a social performance report to the board every six months and discloses the social performance achievements in annual reports.

CD Finance mainly uses three pieces of evidences to measure and demonstrate impacts to potential impact investors:

(1) **Anecdotal evidence**: client stories and testimonials from interviews and field visits; client feedback from annual client satisfaction survey as a proxy for impact and success.
(2) **Standard indicators**: The MIX and the SPTF have developed 11 standard indicators to measure the social performance of financial service providers. The 11 indicators were chosen because they are relevant, easy to obtain, and verify. CD Finance used the 11 indicators to collect social performance data. These 11 indicators are (SPTF 2021):

    - Mission and social goals
    - Governance
    - Range of products and services (financial and non-financial)
    - Social responsibility to clients, including client protection practices
    - Transparency of the costs of services to clients
    - Human resources and staff incentives
    - Social responsibility to the environment
    - Poverty outreach, including the percentage of low-education clients, clients in state-designated poor regions, and clients who never borrowed loans from other formal lending institutions
    - Client outreach by lending methodologies, including women, ethnic minority group outreach
    - Employment creation and enterprises financed
    - Client retention rate.

(3) **External evaluation and rating**: CD Finance also actively invited external evaluation and rating companies to provide assessment and diagnosis, including Planet Social Performance Rating in 2011 and 2015, as well as the Smart

Campaign Client Protection Assessment in 2019. Planet Rating reports demonstrated that CD Finance ranked at the top 44 percentile in terms of social performance among the global MFIs. In 2019, CD Finance was the first financial service provider in China to receive the assessment on both traditional credit and digital credit client protection by the Smart Campaign. The report showed that CD Finance fully met or partially met 98% of over 200 indicators, and only minor improvements were needed to get client protection certification. These reports are very valuable for impact investors to understand the practices, output, outcome, and potential impact.

Although globally there are many client researches on the impact of microfinance, there is a lack of a microfinance impact study specifically focusing on China. CD Finance had long been planning longitudinal research to track the outcome and impact of microfinance on clients' businesses and lives. However, due to practical challenges and resource constraints, CD Finance was not able to launch the research until recently. The research project kicked off in 2021, aiming to track clients' businesses and households over a period of time. CD Finance hopes this research will help address the shortage of customer impact research in both academia and industry in China.

5.3 *How Investors Measure Impacts*

CD Finance's impact investors use various tools, indicator sets, and standards in their practices to measure impacts. The standards and tools are used to assess the impacts of investment ex-ante and monitor results ex-post. Impact investors also use these standards to compare potential impacts across different investment opportunities and to generate lessons learned to improve the selection and design of investment projects.

The most commonly used standard is the U.N Sustainable Development Goals (SDGs). CD Finance's impact investors all indicate which impact themes they target and how those themes are mapped to the SDGs. In addition to SDGs, each investor uses its own measurement framework and tool.

5.3.1 The Rise Fund

In partnership with Y Analytics and The Bridgespan Group (a global social impact advisory firm), The Rise Fund created an evidence-based framework and methodology to assess the potential impact before a single dollar is committed to investment. The frame is called the Impact Multiple of Money (IMM).

Different from other measurement methodology, IMM focuses on "economic quantification of impact" (Gandhi et al. 2018), estimating the value of the social and environmental impacts that are likely to result from each dollar invested. To calculate the IMM, the team would first estimate the potential portfolio company's output. Then they "use the most rigorous academic study available to estimate the expected impact of the company's output" (Gandhi et al. 2018). They would quantify the amount of impact that was attributable to the Rise's investment by multiplying Rise's stake in the potential investee (for example, 10%) by the expected impact. This amount was then divided by the initial Rise investment to calculate the IMM. "If a company did not score above the IMM threshold (2.5x), Rise would not invest it" (Gandhi et al. 2018).

Y Analytics independently conducts ongoing impact assessments for the Rise Fund's portfolio companies throughout the year. To ensure accuracy, KPMG performs an assessment annually on the impact calculations for the companies and the funds. On an annual basis, The Rise Fund reports to its investors for impact generated at both the fund level and on a company-by-company basis.

5.3.2 IFC

The assessment tool IFC developed internally is called the Anticipated Impact Measurement and Monitoring (AIMM) system. IFC scores all of its investment projects for development impact by using the AIMM system. "The AIMM system is now fully integrated into IFC's operations, allowing development impact considerations to be weighed against a range of strategic objectives, including volume, financial return, risk, and thematic priorities" (IFC 2021). This results-measurement framework currently comprises mostly sector-level outcome indicators, including Harmonized Indicators for Private Sector Operations (HIPSO) used by multiple development finance institutions to measure, monitor, and report on development outcomes, including those related to the SDGs (IFC 2021).

5.3.3 HICA

Different from IFC and the Rise Fund, the assessment framework HICA developed is a customized one that integrates financial assessment with impact assessment. The impact assessment tool is based on existing impact assessment standards, such as the Smart Campaign's Client Protection Standard, SPTF's social performance standard, etc. HICA thinks it is not very efficient to operate on dual measuring systems where financial and impact returns are evaluated separately. The customized impact framework (Table 13) includes four main areas and corresponding sub-areas, each assigned with a weight to be combined with financial assessments for calculating the final blended score. The impact performance of portfolio companies is assessed annually and published in an annual report verified by a third party.

Table 13 HICA's impact measurement framework

Area	Sub-areas
Social and environmental performance management system	• Mission, governance, and strategy • Social, environmental, and financial balance • Tracking and monitoring system • HR alignment
Quality of services	• Variety of services • Adequacy of services
Client protection and social responsibility	• Social responsibility toward personnel • Client protection • Green index responsibility community
Outreach	• Area of operations • Target reached

References

Abrams J (2012) Global microfinance ratings comparability. https://www.atlasdata.org/dldocuments/Final%20Report%20Global%20Microfinance%20Ratings%20Comparability.pdf

CGAP (2013) Where do impact investing and microfinance meet? https://www.cgap.org/sites/default/files/Brief-Where-Do-Impact-Investing-and-Microfinance-Meet-June-2013.pdf

Foose L, Folan A (2016) What impact investors can learn from the microfinance industry. https://ssir.org/articles/entry/what_impact_investors_can_learn_from_the_microfinance_industry

Gandhi V, Brumme C, Mehta S (2018) The rise fund: TPG bets big on impact. HBS No 9-318-041. Harvard Business School, Boston

GIIN (2014) The impact programme: annual report 2013. https://thegiin.org/research/publication/the-impact-programme-annual-report-2013

GIIN (2019) Core characteristics of impact investing. https://thegiin.org/assets/Core%20Characteristics_webfile.pdf

GIIN (2021) What is impact investing? https://thegiin.org/impact-investing/need-to-know/#what-is-impact-investing

IFC (2021) Anticipated impact measurement and monitoring. https://www.ifc.org/wps/wcm/connect/topics_ext_content/ifc_external_corporate_site/development+impact/aimm

Impact Principles (2021) The 9 principles. https://www.impactprinciples.org/9-principles

Lieberman I (2020) The growth and commercial evolution of microfinance. In: The future of microfinance. Brookings Institution Press, Washington, D.C.

Pandit V, Tamhane T (2018) A closer look at impact investing. McKinsey Quarterly. https://www.mckinsey.com/industries/private-equity-and-principal-investors/our-insights/a-closer-look-at-impact-investing

SPTF (2021) The universal standards for social performance management. https://sptf.info/universal-standards-for-spm/universal-standards

Twersky F, Nelson J, Ractcliffe A (2010) A guide to actionable measurement. The gates foundation. https://docs.gatesfoundation.org/documents/guide-to-actionable-measurement.pdf

Warwick M, Dileo P, Polak P (2015) What impact investors can learn from microfinance? https://www.devex.com/news/what-impact-investors-can-learn-from-microfinance-85516

Conclusions and Recommendations

The impact investing industry is still nascent in China and there are several bottlenecks constraining its development. It is important to acknowledge these barriers so that we can better identify the opportunities to collaborate and address these challenges systematically. On the several key issues in the field of impact investing listed, some of the main findings of this book are as follows.

(1) **Definition and Understanding of Impact Investing**

There is no widely accepted definition of impact investing in China. Some equal impact investing with SRI and ESG Investing. Some thought impact investing pays only sub-commercial returns. Despite the fact that much progress has been achieved globally in terms of impact investing best practices and standards, few have been regularly and systematically introduced to China. A couple of investors interviewed expressed the concerns that many foreign-coined concepts have challenges in achieving universal understanding in China. For example, there is no widely accepted definition for "financial inclusion" in China after almost 15 years of industry development.

A lack of common understanding not only creates confusion and misconception, but also deters potential investments. As shown in CD Finance's case, it takes extra efforts for them to convince domestic investors without deep sector knowledge on how they adopt a market-based approach to address societal issues and how they differ from those irresponsible lenders.

(2) **An Ecosystem of Impact Investing in China**

What impact investing can learn from microfinance is: for impact investing to become a mainstream practice, it needs an ecosystem including enabling environment, industry builders, and different players such as standard-setters, government bodies, collaboration networks, corporations, investors, and philanthropy organizations. Currently, there is a lack of enabling environment for impact investing in China. The regulatory framework does not support or motivate investment managers who seek to create impact alongside a financial return. There is also a lack of awareness

Finance Center for South-South Cooperation, *Impact Investing*,
https://doi.org/10.1007/978-981-99-4935-9_5

and practices to build the industry, supporting the impact investing reduce risks, better leverage capital as well as providing integral support to social businesses. CD Finance has greatly benefited from the global microfinance ecosystem, such as learning from the global best practices, obtaining the grant and capital from global donors and investors, and receiving ratings and assessments from international rating companies, etc. As proved by the commercialization of microfinance, ecosystem building would significantly promote industry transparency, establish best practices, and hence fuel investments in the sector.

(3) **Investment Opportunities and Startup Incubators**

Impact investors commonly have trouble in finding high-quality social enterprises with strong potential of profitability and impacts in China. On the one hand, there is an insufficient number of mission-driven or social enterprises in China. An impact investor interviewed mentioned that she has visited many so-called "social businesses" seeking impact investing, but the majority of them did not intentionally pursue social impact or have a good understanding of social sectors. On the other hand, many social enterprises with strong knowledge of social problems lack the business skills and capital to scale the social business and yield strong financial returns to attract investors.

In the early stage, the young social businesses need resources (training, guidance, grant, subsidy, network, etc.) to build institutional capacity, strengthen business models, and deploy innovative technology. For instance, the early investors of CD Finance were largely from philanthropy organizations and DFIs. For startup businesses, they need concessionary impact investors who are willing to take a higher risk and know how to identify early-stage social businesses with strong potential. It is very challenging to secure investment without an experienced team and a proven track record of profitability and impacts, but it is also a struggle to acquire experienced talent and build a track record without significant investment in the seed stage. The industry needs venture philanthropy and concessionary impact investors to overcome the chicken and egg conundrum.

(4) **Impact Measurement Methods and Standards**

Measuring social impact is a challenge for both investors and investees. For investees, the resource requirement is burdensome. For investors, they are not sure how to track the social return on investments. Globally with the market of impact investing maturing, impact management and measurement (IMM) practices have grown increasingly sophisticated. But in China there are still very few researches and resources committed to impact measurement. Lack of standards and tools also makes it difficult to compare investment opportunities and to allocate capital. All of these will seriously affect the credibility of the industry.

Looking at the development of impact investing internationally and in China, four key lessons for impact investing in China can be summarized, which will help tackle the bottlenecks mentioned above and accelerate the future growth of impact investing in China.

First, a trusted and influential network or knowledge-sharing platform of Impact investing in China needs to build, such as a Chinese version of GIIN. It takes much more effort to correct misconceptions than to build the right understanding from the beginning. This network or knowledge-sharing platform would serve as the champion of impact investing in China. As the role of GIIN in the global impact investing industry and CGAP in the financial inclusion industry, the network would define the key terms, offer information, tools, and resources that fill knowledge gaps, and tirelessly strive to increase the awareness and understanding in the industry through campaigns, industry research, training, publications, networking events, etc. The network would serve as a bridge between investors looking for high-impact opportunities and social businesses tackling social and environmental problems. It would convene impact investors to facilitate knowledge exchange, build the evidence base, and produce tools for investors to effectively select investment opportunities and manage the portfolio. It would also help reduce barriers for social ventures to get access to and secure impact investing capital. It would need to play a leading role in building a solid infrastructure that helps accelerate the development of the impact investing industry in China.

Second, the government should encourage startup incubation and help the development of social enterprises. The industry needs concessionary investors and venture philanthropy organizations to take the greater risk or accept the lower returns to invest in promising social businesses that do not yet attract non-concessionary impact investment capital due to higher risk, an unproven track record, or an uncertain return timeline. As social businesses establish track records and are prepared to scale and expand, non-concessionary impact investors and mainstream traditional investors would increasingly join the force. The industry also needs investors and philanthropy organizations to provide grants and subsidies along the capital to support nascent social businesses to build institutional capacity. Accelerators and incubators can be established to help early-stage social businesses by providing mentorship, incubation, technical assistance, and seed capital. The importance of contributing resources to build the institutional capacity of nascent social businesses needs to be raised among domestic donors and investors in China. Impact investors also need to hire sector specialists and deepen the sector knowledge, which will help investors identify the promising opportunity for investment that others would pass up and miss. Impact investors need to identify the visionary social entrepreneurs who can recognize unjust social issues, identify business opportunities, inspire changes, and take direct actions. Resources need to be committed to increasing the capacity of social entrepreneurs too.

Third, China's impact management and measurement (IMM) tools should be developed. The industry needs collaborated efforts and significant resources to develop a wealth of measurement tools and frameworks. According to the GIIN survey (Bass et al. 2020), impact investors take no single approach to IMM as often one tool is not enough to cover all of the sectors they invest. They use various tools, frameworks, and standards according to their preferences, capabilities, and specific sectors for investments. For example, social performance standards set by SPTF focus on financial inclusion. There are also other measurement systems and indicators

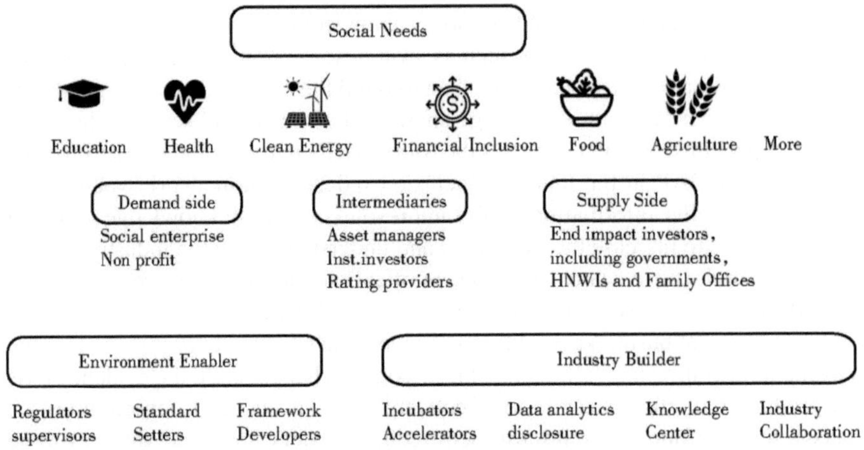

Fig. 1 Ecosystem of impact investing. *Source* Illustration by author

specifically for one or multiple sectors such as agriculture, climate, health, education, energy, etc. Significant resources need to be committed in China in creating impact measurement methods and demonstrating evidence of impacts in different sectors. A knowledge center can consolidate IMM resources into one searchable database and establish comparability among different systems and tools so that it brings greater transparency and comparability to the performance of impact investing.

Fourth, China should promote the building of an impact investing ecosystem. The ecosystem can start with networks that simply exchange information and gradually evolve into more substantive alliances that coordinate investment resources, enable investment environment, build industry evidence and practices, and connect impact investors with social ventures. Besides investor and social businesses, the ecosystem needs environment enablers and industry builders. Environment enablers include regulators, impact framework developers, and performance standard setters. Industry builders include industry networks, social business accelerators and incubators, knowledge-sharing platforms, data analytics, and disclosure platforms. Philanthropy, impact investors, and government can play catalytic roles in committing resources to build the ecosystem (see Fig. 1).

At the time of conducting this research, the pandemic is continuing around the world. The COVID-19 crisis has reinforced the urgency of addressing social and environmental challenges. We have seen the increased interest in the impact investing market and heightened shareholder pressure around social responsibility. Looking ahead, with increasing enthusiasm in entrepreneurship and creative activism among Gen Z in China, we have strong reasons to believe that we will see an exponential rise in innovations to address the imminent social and climate challenges in China. We will also see an increasing number of impact investing that follows the global trend. Impact investors, social businesses, regulators, and philanthropy organizations must collaborate to systematically leverage the power of capital to address and ultimately solve the critical social and environmental problems in China.

Reference

Bass R, Dithrich H, Sunderji S, Nova N (2020) The state of impact measurement and management practice. https://thegiin.org/assets/GIIN_State%20of%20Impact%20Measurement%20and%20Management%20Practice_Second%20Edition.pdf

Appendix

Definitions come consolidated by Impact Management Project except for corporate social responsibility, green finance, impact investing, and social enterprise:

B Lab

B Lab is a nonprofit that serves a global movement of people using business as a force for good. B Lab's initiatives include B Corp Certification, administration of the B Impact Management programs and software, and advocacy for governance structures like the benefit corporation (B Lab).

Base of Pyramid

The Base of the Pyramid (BOP) theory suggests that new business opportunities lie in designing and distributing goods and services for poor communities. The idea is espoused by influential US business school academics CK Prahalad and Stuart Hart, who argue that companies can help eradicate poverty by providing goods and services for the 4bn people who live on less than $2 a day—this group is known as the base of the pyramid (Financial Times Lexicon).

Cleantech

Alternatively referred to as environmental technology or green tech, this term is used to describe a collection of modern technologies and approaches that maximize human, environmental, and economic benefits. Specifically, green tech utilizes advancements of modern environmental science, biotechnology, and engineering to provide products and services in a way that least degrades natural resources and in some cases, regenerates them. Common examples of green tech include materials recycling; utilization of solar, wind, and other renewable energy sources for power; biological water treatment and greywater recycling; biofuels; and energy-conserving electronics (Presidio Graduate School, Sustainability Dictionary).

Corporate Social Responsibility

Corporate social responsibility (CSR) is a self-regulating business model that helps a company be socially accountable—to itself, its stakeholders, and the public. By

Finance Center for South-South Cooperation, *Impact Investing*,
https://doi.org/10.1007/978-981-99-4935-9

practicing corporate social responsibility, also called corporate citizenship, companies can be conscious of the kind of impact they are having on all aspects of society, including economic, social, and environmental.

To engage in CSR means that, in the ordinary course of business, a company is operating in ways that enhance society and the environment instead of contributing negatively to them (Investopedia).

Development Finance Institution

The term "development finance institutions" (DFI) encompasses not only government development banks, but also nongovernmental micro-finance organizations that match grants to attempt to promote community development, decentralization of power, and local empowerment. Measures of the social cost of DFIs that receive public funds help to check whether DFIs are good uses of public funds, i.e., if the social benefit of a DFI exceeds the social cost, then public funds are indeed well-spent, further improving social welfare (World Bank).

Environmental, Social, and Governance Criteria

A set of standards for a company's operations that socially conscious investors use to screen investments. Environmental criteria look at how a company performs as a steward of the natural environment. Social criteria examine how a company manages relationships with its employees, suppliers, customers, and the communities where it operates. Governance deals with a company's leadership, executive pay, audits, and internal controls, and shareholder rights. Investors who want to purchase securities that have been screened for ESG criteria can do so through socially responsible mutual funds and exchange-traded funds (Investopedia).

Financial First

"Financial first" means investors who prioritize the financial return objective over the social or environmental objectives of an investment. This group tends to include commercial investors seeking investments that offer market-rate returns and also yield social or environmental good. Also included in this group are investors who are required to uphold a fiduciary standard and are therefore unable to make investments that lack the potential to yield market-rate returns (TriLinc Global Impact Investing Glossary).

General Partner

One of the co-owners of an unincorporated business (organized as a general partnership) who has control of the firm and, unlike limited or nominal partner, has unlimited personal liability for the firm's debts. Actions taken by one general partner are binding upon the other general partners. Also called full partner (BusinessDictionary.com).

Global Impact Investing Network

A nonprofit organization dedicated to increasing the scale and effectiveness of impact investing around the world (Global Impact Investing Network).

Global Impact Investing Rating System

A project of B Lab that assesses the social and environmental impact (but not the financial performance) of companies and funds, using a rating approach analogous to Morningstar investment rankings or rating agency credit risk ratings (TriLinc Global Impact Investing Glossary).

Green Finance

Green finance can be understood as financing of investments that provide environmental benefits in the broader context of environmentally sustainable development. These environmental benefits include, for example, reductions in air, water and land pollution, reductions in greenhouse gas (GHG) emissions, improved energy efficiency while utilizing existing natural resources, as well as mitigation of and adaptation to climate change and their co-benefits. Green finance involves efforts to internalize environmental externalities and adjust risk perceptions in order to boost environmentally friendly investments and reduce environmentally harmful ones. Green finance covers a wide range of financial institutions and asset classes and includes both public and private finance. Green finance involves the effective management of environmental risks across the financial system (G20 Green Finance Synthesis Report).

High Net Worth Individual

HNWI is a classification used by the financial services industry to denote an individual or a family with high net worth. Although there is no precise definition of how rich somebody must be to fit into this category, high net worth is generally quoted in terms of liquid assets over a certain figure. The exact amount differs by financial institution and region, but the most commonly quoted figure for membership in the high-net-worth club is $1 million in liquid financial assets (Investopedia).

Impact First

Impact first investors are targeting social or environmental good as their primary objective, above achieving a financial return. This may mean accepting a below-market rate of return in order to reach tougher social/environmental goals that are seemingly not achievable through mainstream investment or philanthropic activities (TriLinc Global Impact Investing Glossary).

Impact Investing

Impact investments are investments made with the intention to generate positive, measurable social and environmental impact alongside a financial return. Impact investments can be made in both emerging and developed markets and target a range of returns from below market to market rate, depending on investors' strategic goals. There are four key elements:

- Intentionality: Impact investments intentionally contribute to social and environmental solutions. This differentiates them from other strategies such as ESG investing, responsible investing, and screening strategies.

- Financial returns: Impact investments are expected to generate a financial return on capital or, at minimum, a return of capital. This distinguishes them from philanthropy.
- Range of asset classes: Impact investments can be made across asset classes.
- Impact measurement: A hallmark of impact investing is the commitment of the investor to measure and report the social and environmental performance of underlying investments.

(Global Impact Investing Network).

Impact Management

No clear, authoritative definition currently exists. See commentary. The Impact Management Project describes impact management as learning about–and improving–effects experienced by people and the planet (Impact Management Project).

Impact Measurement

Measuring and managing the process of creating social and environmental impact in order to maximize and optimize it (European Venture Philanthropy Association).

Impact Reporting and Investment Standards

The Impact Reporting and Investment Standards (IRIS) provide a common reporting language to describe the social and environmental performance and ensure uniform measurement and articulation of impact across portfolios. The IRIS initiative defines terms to enable consistent reporting and allows benchmarking of data across companies, funds, investment portfolios, and other organizations by serving as a repository for aggregated IRIS-compliant data. IRIS is an initiative of the Global Impact Investing Network (Middlebury Institute of International Studies).

Limited Partner

Limited partner (LP) is one of the co-owners of a business organized as limited partnership who (unlike a general partner) does not participate in the management of the firm and has limited personal liability for the firm's debts. Also called nominal partner (BusinessDictionary.com).

Market-Rate Investment

No clear, authoritative definition was found. See commentary. The term is used to differentiate an investment that expects to receive an average or typical financial rate of return for a given level of risk (i.e., a market-rate return) from an investment that expects to receive a below-average financial return but generates positive social and/or environmental impacts (Impact Management Project).

Microfinance

Microfinance is a type of banking service that is provided to unemployed or low-income individuals, or groups who otherwise have no other access to financial services. Ultimately, the goal of microfinance is to give low-income people an opportunity to become self-sufficient by providing a way to save money, borrow money, and get insurance (TriLinc Global Impact Investing Glossary).

Mission Related Investment

An investment made using assets from a foundation's endowment that seeks to create social impact as well as typically risk-adjusted financial returns (TriLinc Global Impact Investing Glossary).

Private Equity

Capital that is not noted on a public exchange. Private equity is composed of funds and investors that directly invest in private companies or that engage in buyouts of public companies, resulting in the delisting of public equity. Institutional and retail investors provide the capital for private equity, and the capital can be utilized to fund new technology, make acquisitions, expand working capital, and bolster and solidify a balance sheet (Investopedia).

Responsible Investment

Responsible investment is an investment strategy that seeks to generate both financial and sustainable value. It consists of a set of investment approaches that integrate environmental, social and governance (ESG) and ethical issues into financial analysis and decision-making. Responsible investment goes by many names—it is variously referred to as socially responsible investing (SRI), ethical investing, sustainable investing, triple-bottom-line investing, green investing—but underlying these differing names is a common theme focused on long-term value creation. Value in this context refers not only to economic value, but to the broader values of fairness, justice, and environmental sustainability (Financial Times Lexicon).

Social Enterprise

Any organization in any sector that uses earned income strategies to pursue a double bottom line or a triple bottom line, either alone (as a social sector business) or as part of a mixed revenue stream that includes charitable contributions and public sector subsidies (The Institute for Social Entrepreneurs).

Triple Bottom Line

Triple bottom line is a phrase introduced in 1994 by John Elkington and later used in his 1997 book "Cannibals with Forks: The Triple Bottom Line Of 21st Century Business," which seeks to broaden the focus on the financial bottom line by businesses to include social and environmental responsibilities. A triple bottom line measures a company's degree of social responsibility, its economic value and its environmental impact. A key challenge with the triple bottom line, according to Elkington, is the difficulty of measuring the social and environmental bottom lines, which necessitates the three separate accounts being evaluated on their own merits (Investopedia).

Venture Philanthropy

A high-engagement and long-term approach to generating societal impact through three practices:

- Tailored financing: Using a range of financing mechanisms (including grants, debt, and equity hybrid financing) tailored to the needs of the organization supported.
- Organizational Support: Added-value support services that VPOs offer to investees (SPOs) to strengthen the SPO's organizational resilience and financial sustainability by developing skills or improving structures and processes.
- Impact measurement and management: Measuring and managing the process of creating social impact in order to maximize and optimize it (European Venture Philanthropy Association 2012).

Bibliography

Allen F, Qian J, Zhang C, Zhao M (2013) China's financial system: opportunities and challenges. Fan J, Morck R (eds) Capitalizing China. Massachusetts, Cambridge. National Bureau of Economic Research, pp 63–143

Asian Development Bank (2014) Asia SME monitor 2013. Asia Development Bank

Asian Venture Philanthropy Network (2019a) AVPN annual report. https://avpn.asia/insights/annual-review-2019/

Bloomberg News (2019) China is mulling tougher rules on private equity, hedge funds. Bloomberg, 7 March. https://www.bloomberg.com/news/articles/2019-03-07/china-said-to-mull-tougher-rules-on-private-equity-hedge-funds

Bridges Fund Management (2017) The bridges spectrum of capital how we define the sustainable and impact investment market. Bridges Fund Management. https://www.bridgesfundmanagement.com/wp-content/uploads/2017/08/Bridges-Spectrum-of-Capital-screen.pdf

British Council (n.d.) Social Enterprise. https://www.britishcouncil.org/society/social-enterprise

Case J (2017) Bringing the last decade of impact investing to life: an interactive timeline. Case Foundation. https://casefoundation.org/blog/bringing-last-decade-impact-investing-life-interactive-timeline

Chang M (2019) Charitable giving in china-from passion to impact. Cheung Kong graduate school of business knowledge. http://knowledge.ckgsb.edu.cn/2019/10/25/csr/charitable-giving-china-impact/

Charities and Foundations (2018) CAF world giving index 2018. Charities and Foundations. https://www.cafonline.org/about-us/publications/2018-publications/caf-world-giving-index-2018

China Development Brief (2016) English Translation of China's new law on overseas NGOs. China Development Brief. http://www.chinadevelopmentbrief.cn/articles/the-peoples-republic-of-chinas-law-on-the-management-of-the-activities-of-overseas-ngos-within-mainland-china/

Emerging Markets Private Equity Association (2020) 2019 data. Emerging Markets Private Equity Association

European Venture Philanthropy Association (2012) European Venture Philanthropy and Social Investment 2011/2012. https://www.philanthropy-impact.org/sites/default/files/downloads/Online_EVPA-Survey_2011_2012.pdf

Fang W (2019) Interviewed by Rae Winborn. EHong Capital Interview

Feng C (2017) The NGO law in China and its impact on overseas funded NGOs. Cosmopol Civil Soc Interdiscipl J 9(3):95–105

Full J (2019) Interviewed by Rae Winborn. YouChange Foundation Interview No 1

Gan N (2017) Why foreign NGOs are struggling with new Chinese law. South China Morning Post. https://www.scmp.com/news/china/policies-politics/article/2097923/why-foreign-ngos-are-struggling-new-chinese-law

Finance Center for South-South Cooperation, *Impact Investing*,
https://doi.org/10.1007/978-981-99-4935-9

Geng L, Li Y, Wang Y (2019) Seeking common ground. Stanford Social Innovation Review. https://ssir.org/articles/entry/seeking_common_ground

Gilbert S, Zhao L (2017) The knowns and unknowns of China's green finance, contributing paper for the sustainable infrastructure imperative: financing for better growth and development. New Climate Economy, London and Washington, D. C. http://newclimateeconomy.report/misc/working-papers

Han J (2017a) Impact investing: a brief history of ten years (2007—2017), December 12, 2017. China Development Brief. http://www.chinadevelopmentbrief.org.cn/news-20594.html

Hsu D (2019) Interviewed by Rae Winborn. Bits X Bites Investment Interview

Hu J (2019) Interviewed by Rae Winborn. YouChange Foundation Interview No 2

IFC (2018) IFC's contribution to the sustainable development goals. https://www.ifc.org/wps/wcm/connect/1433afde-d252-42f2-bbd9-839e30a69947/201803_IFCs-contribution-to-the-SDGs_v1.pdf?MOD=AJPERES&CVID=m9zP1Y-

IFC (2020) Growing impact: new insights into the practice of impact investing. https://sptf.info/component/content/article?id=120:mix-sp-indicators

Jaquier J (2016) Catalyzing wealth for change: guide to impact investing (executive summary). http://www.ebanimpact.org/wp-content/uploads/2016/10/Guide-to-Impact-Investing-Executive-Summary.pdf

Latham and Watkins (2019) China introduces new foreign investment law, negative lists, and encouraged industries catalogue. Client Alert White Paper, Latham and Watkins. https://www.lw.com/thoughtLeadership/china-introduces-new-foreign-investment-law-negative-lists-and-encouraged-industries-catalogue

Lee E (2019) Interviewed by Rae Winborn. LGT Interview

Li D (2017) How china's social enterprises can prosper alongside the country's state-run businesses. World Economic Forum. https://www.weforum.org/agenda/2017/06/how-china-s-social-enterprises-can-prosper-alongside-the-country-s-state-run-businesses/

Lin S (2018) China's new charity law: a new era of charitable trusts. Trusts Trustees 24(8):768–777

Lu Q (2019) Interviewed by Rae Winborn. Tsing Capital Interview

Lu Y (2017) Why giving is harder than earning: Philanthropy in China. The Economist, https://www.economist.com/china/2018/09/06/why-do-people-in-china-give-so-little-to-charity

Ma L (2016) Who's the biggest giver? Top 10 philanthropists in China and the United States. South China Morning Post. https://www.scmp.com/news/china/money-wealth/article/1922705/whos-biggest-giver-top-10-philanthropists-china-and-united

National People's Congress (2016) Charity Law of the PRC. Translated from Chinese by China Development Brief. http://www.chinadevelopmentbrief.cn/wp-content/uploads/2016/04/Charity-Law-CDB-Translation.pdf

Nicholas J (2019) Interviewed by Rae Winborn. Impact Experience Interview

O'Flynn P, Higdon GL (2019) Is participatory impact investing the antidote to "impact washing"? https://www.ids.ac.uk/opinions/is-participatory-impact-investing-the-antidote-to-impact-washing

Ren D (2017) Stronger efforts called for at educating China's 100 million retail investors. South China Morning Post. https://www.scmp.com/business/companies/article/2122659/stronger-efforts-called-educating-chinas-100-million-retail

Silby W (2019) Interviewed by Rae Winborn. Calvert Impact Interview

SPTF (2021) MIX Social Performance Indicators. https://sptf.info/component/content/article?id=120:mix-sp-indicators

Tan Y (2020) Interviewed by Rae Winborn. Narada Foundation Investment Interview

Tiftik E, Mahmood K (2019) High and rising debt levels: should we worry? Global debt monitor slide deck. Institute of International Finance. https://www.iif.com/Portals/0/Files/content/GDM_Aug2019_vf.pdf

Tsai K (2016) When shadow banking can be productive: financing small and medium enterprises in China. J Dev Stud 53(12):2005–2028. https://doi.org/10.1080/00220388.2016.1228877

United Nations Development Programme (2018) China Charity Law Handbook. UNDP. https://www.cn.undp.org/content/china/en/home/library/democratic_governance/handbook-of-charity-law-of-the-peoples-republic-of-china.html

Wang O, Bray C (2019) China's P2P lending market could be decimated this year amid Beijing crackdown. South China Morning Post. https://www.scmp.com/economy/china-economy/article/3006170/chinas-p2p-lending-market-could-be-decimated-year-amid

World Bank (2018) Worldwide Governance Indicators. World Bank. https://databank.worldbank.org/source/worldwide-governance-indicators

World Economic Forum (2018) The inclusive development index. World Economic Forum. http://www3.weforum.org/docs/WEF_Forum_IncGrwth_2018.pdf

Xiao H (2019) Interviewed by Rae Winborn. Mana Impact Investment Interview

Xu C (2019) Interviewed by Rae Winborn. Venture Avenue Interview

Yu X (2016) China to force out 2 000 private asset management companies. South China Morning Post. https://www.scmp.com/business/markets/article/1940714/china-force-out-2000-private-asset-management-companies

Zhang T, Ge Y, Zhao R (2012) Creating the Chinese Dream: a practitioner's guide to impact investing in China's green SMEs. China Impact Fund

Zhao M, Guo S (2017) CFPA Microfinance: Social enterprise in transformation, GC-16-004-CE, Shanghai. CEIBS.

Zhu R, Li M (2019) CD finance: innovation in poverty alleviation through microfinance. 2019-9-5-439-1. Shanghai. CKGSB

MIX
Papier aus verantwortungsvollen Quellen
Paper from responsible sources
FSC® C105338

FSC
www.fsc.org

If you have any concerns about our products,
you can contact us on
ProductSafety@springernature.com

In case Publisher is established outside the EU,
the EU authorized representative is:
Springer Nature Customer Service Center GmbH
Europaplatz 3, 69115 Heidelberg, Germany

Printed by Libri Plureos GmbH
in Hamburg, Germany